The Cash Cage

Booklocker.com, Inc.
2004

http://www.thecashcage.com

The Cash Cage

Corey Deitz

Dedicated to my wife, Chris, and my boys, David and Eric.

…And to every listener who has ever allowed me to spend time with them.

Introduction

It is not as easy as it would seem to condense a good portion of one's life down into mere words. Each word springs from the same alphabet and each sentence is printed in the same color. Almost every book ever written pulls from the same universe of words; the words are just arranged differently to tell a unique story. It took me two years to arrange all the words in this book. The challenge to any writer is to sculpt each paragraph in just the proper fashion so all the words leave you with the feeling as though you have had a very special experience.

Writing about the good times is easy. The hard part is being willing to look your deepest regrets square in the face, admit your most hollow failures and share some of the ugly truths about yourself and your life which you are under no obligation to ever divulge.

Step behind my microphone and we'll walk together through the back hallways of some great and not-so-great American radio stations during both highly successful and terribly devastating times. For the average reader, it will be a journey into a sometimes glamorous and definitely cutthroat world few are admitted to. If you have spent some time working in Radio, my experiences will no doubt trigger some deja vu - and possibly seizures. I'm sorry about that. Keep your meds handy. If you are new to this business, you might wonder why you didn't go for that middle-level management job at McDonalds.

If you want to work and succeed in Radio, you must be prepared to move. It is a volatile business and quite unforgiving. You are only as good as your latest ratings and sometimes, even that's just not good enough. I have lived in big cities like Chicago, on a homestead of 10 acres in rural Virginia, and everywhere else in between. The places I loved most were the ones I could not remain in because that luxury does not always exist in Radio.

Counting interim rentals, hotels, apartments, and houses, I have lived in 34 different places since beginning my career. I've spent time in cities and towns I did not like, left behind friends I would not see again, often uprooted the family I love, and did whatever I had to do to stay employed because I love this business and my survival instincts are strong.

I have been fortunate to have spent all of my professional life doing something many people only dream of. Imagine going to a job each day where others choose to listen to you because they think you are interesting, funny, possibly intelligent or maybe even clever. That's a good job - even if they're all mistaken!

For my pleasure and trouble, I have been handsomely rewarded. Radio hasn't made me rich, but I have lived well. I have lived better than many. I have been lucky. I have survived in a business where one day you are exalted and the next day you are cannibalized. The good times have been many and the inevitable bad times are just part of the bargain.

That is the deal you make with this devil.

Chapter 1

When I was a boy, there was a radio by the side of my bed. I have no specific memory of it ever being given to me or even placed there. It was rectangular, off-white, made of hard plastic, and about the size of child's lunch-box. There were three small knobs attached to the very bottom, aligned and evenly spaced. The one on the far left turned it on and off. The second knob, to its immediate right, adjusted the volume. The third one, the largest of the three, pointed to a series of numbers that surrounded the perimeter of the knob in a crescent shape from left to right.

It was just an AM radio, but it ushered into my world an exciting mix of Top 40 hit music, jingles, and deejays, all peppered by commercials for a 24-hour clothing store located somewhere off the New Jersey Turnpike and a man named "Crazy Eddie" who sold car stereos and televisions in New York City.

My earliest memories of listening to that radio are at night. Though I was supposed to be sleeping, most nights, after my mother and father were assured I was safely tucked in, I would carefully reach over onto my nightstand and gently click it on. I kept the volume so low I had to strain to hear it. Usually, I would lie motionless, listening intently to a disc jockey named "Cousin Brucie" on WABC-AM in New York City. His name was a little perplexing to me because I had cousins in New York yet, I had not met this one - at least I had never seen him at any family gatherings. However, he seemed kind enough and in my mind, it would have been just fine if we were related.

Although I did not know it at the time, "Cousin Brucie", was the alter ego of Bruce Morrow, an on-air persona created simply to appeal to teenagers and anyone else on the verge of being one. His plan worked perfectly and I listened every night as my "cousin" played wonderful songs and talked to me in between them. We had a splendid time until I fell asleep.

Years later, when I worked in Cleveland, Ohio, I finally met Bruce Morrow while I was broadcasting from the opening of the Rock and Roll Hall of Fame. I was on the air and he ambled by our broadcast booth accompanied by another famous deejay, Norm N. Nite. I interviewed them both. We took one of those photos where everyone puts their arms around each other and smiles as if they are the best of friends. Little did Morrow realize how long I really had known him nor that he my earliest inspiration. I still have the photo hanging in my home office. Its funny how life completes some circles when you least expect it.

I was 11 or 12 the first time I tried being a deejay. I was in the basement of a friend's home, sitting on the floor and swapping vinyl 45-rpm records on and off a mechanical turntable. I would make up stuff to say in order to fill up the intro time of each song before the vocals began. I was fairly certain these were the only skills you needed to be on the radio. Yes, I was quite sure that the important thing was to talk until the singing started. Therefore, I practiced quite earnestly.

Somewhere in my early teens, I decided I should probably be a rock star. Don't we all? So, I put my radio aspirations on hold and began writing songs and playing guitar in a band. I figured it would actually be better to make the songs people heard on the radio than to spin them. In time, I let go of rock stardom, opting instead to continue my writing.

That was the plan: attend the small college near home, save Mom and Dad a fortune, get a degree in English, and then struggle for years with little income and great hopes in pursuit of pure poetry or palatable prose. (See, even now I cannot help but abuse alliteration. It is the curse of all former English majors.)

It did not quite work out that way. Halfway through my freshman year my early fascination with being a deejay was suddenly rekindled through a chance invitation to the campus radio station. It was suddenly quite clear: I was meant to be on the radio.

When I first announced this new epiphany to my parents, it was a bit uncomfortable.

"Mom? Dad? I've made a decision. I'm going to become a disc jockey."

They both looked at me as if they were wondering what kind of skill that actually required.

I was thinking, "Please don't ask me." However, it was too late.

"What kind of skill does that actually require," asked my father. (By the way, that's Dad-code for "so you're going to be a bum". He was trying to be diplomatic.)

Skills? I really couldn't tell him. I didn't think he would buy "filling up the intro time of each song before the vocals began".

He sat there, pleasantly nodding his head as I attempted some kind of explanation. I'm sure my words were simply background noise. By now, he was probably adding up in his head what it was going to cost to send me wherever I was going next.

I'm sure he was grateful I was the last child he had to deal with. I was born late in my parent's life. I was the baby of the family.

My father, Morris, was the son of Russian Jews who immigrated to America around 1910 and settled on Flatbush Avenue in Brooklyn, New York. His father became a successful businessman in women's underwear. I don't mean wearing it, I mean selling it. (Of course, today a man can still make a name for himself in women's underwear. Just look at Eddie Izzard, Dennis Rodman, or Ru Paul.) However, before my Dad could enjoy the benefit of his father's success, my grandmother tossed my grandfather out of the house and subsequently divorced him because of his sexual ramblings with other women. The old man pleaded with her to take him back but she would have none of it. Her pride stood firm.

My grandfather was banished from the household and my Dad never saw him again. The grandfather I never met died alone, many years later in California. Someone sent my father a clipping of the newspaper obituary. It was one of the few times I ever saw him cry. He always resented my grandmother because without his father, my father and his three other brothers had to grow up fast and begin earning money for the family. Life was hard.

My father was a child of the depression and never forgot the worth of a dollar. He would do almost any job for any amount of money because payment-in-hand fed more mouths than pride-in-heart. Even later in life, after becoming a successful businessman, he always looked for extra ways to earn a buck. Retirement didn't even interfere with his credo. He insisted on doing odd jobs for payment until he passed away at 78. The fear that he might one day wind up desperately short of money never left his tortured subconscious, a deep scar leftover from his childhood.

3

My mother, Sophie, was the daughter of Polish immigrants. They died of consumption when she was a very small child and she was shuttled off to an orphanage. At bedtime, the caretakers would place the next day's clothing at the foot of each child's bed. Late at night, when all were asleep, Mom would sneak around, substituting her garments for the outfit that most pleased her, no matter what bed it had been placed in front of. She never forgot her poverty and for the rest of her life had an obsession with clothing, material possessions and her appearance.

When it comes to money, my values were directly molded from my father and mother's reaction to their childhood. Their mantra was simple: earn it, earn more of it and then after you earn it, save it. That is exactly what I have done from the time I was small.

Earn it, earn more of it and then after you earn it, save it.

So, when my father questioned my decision to enter broadcasting, what he really wanted to know was what kind of living could I expect to make? Hell, I didn't know. In fact, I didn't even know what I needed to learn. However, the truth is Radio doesn't demand too many skills.

Some people go to specialized broadcast schools to learn "radio skills". Others go to college and major in it. Many students get their foot in the door by earning college credits for internships. Still others, through a quirk of fate, accidentally find themselves doing odd jobs at radio stations, which eventually lead to better opportunities and even full careers. There seems to be no particular prerequisites or qualifications necessary to be on the radio nor any rhyme or reason for having success at it. Given this, I have somehow managed to be a radio personality for all my working adult life - which is like not really having a job at all.

Let's be clear about this: I don't really work for a living - at least not by any reasonable definition. None of us does. And if anyone in Radio claims he works - he's lying. I mean, you can't really call this work. It's not like digging ditches on a road repair crew or pushing a lawn mower around for a landscaping company. Most people produce something tangible at their job: a report, a spreadsheet, grommets for tarps or finely honed 6-layer-burritos that make the general public want to run for the border. I talk a lot and after four hours on the air each morning - unless you were recording it - you wouldn't even know I had rolled out of bed in the middle-of-the-night to show up for work. It's all very conveniently gone and dispersed on the backs of electro-magnetic waves that travel invisibly through the ether.

In the end, there's no product you can hold or look at. Nothing to put on a shelf and sell at a store. No evidence I've even done anything once I walk out of the studio. There is no inventory to shelve, no products to label, nothing to ship. All I have to do is show up, open my mouth and get people to like me - or at least hate me enough to listen anyway. Either is fine. Nevertheless, in the end, I'm just breathing, not working.

My typical workday: spend two hours on the Internet preparing my show (not work), talk during the course of four hours on the air (not work), maybe a few tasks after my shift (still not work) and go home. Sometimes I am asked to show up at station function or concert to emcee or host. Other than that, I'm left to my own devices. Should someone outside of the station, like a client, request the pleasure of my company for a remote broadcast or appearance, I'm usually paid a talent fee of $100-an-hour. What the fuck are they thinking? You figure it out.

Therefore, it begs the question: how is it I have a contract to work doing something, which can't be defined as such.

It's puzzling - which may explain why some people in management don't get along very well with talent. I think there's a certain amount of jealousy between management and on-air performers. After all, they have to work and we don't. They sit through tedious business meetings, create impressive budgets with lots of colors, schmooze clients at lunch, and put in long hours. They have to act like adults and wear business attire. I am not required to do either.

If my theory is correct and management is jealous, at the same time it also knows it needs talent, even if it can't resolve the inner conflict of giving us money for what appears to be very little effort. Can you imagine paying somebody thousands and thousands of dollars each year for them to show up and appear not to work? This is the ultimate irony for a businessperson. It's true: repeatedly, people who own or run radio stations have actually promised me in writing and on real paper that they would pay me for several years to do something that does not resemble work. Not only that; at least three times in my career, companies have paid me thousands of dollars not only to *not* work, but also to *not work while staying home.*

Is this a great country or what?

You will soon notice if you haven't already sometimes I capitalize Radio and sometimes I don't. This is not the result of sloppiness, bad proof reading or lousy editing. To me, Radio is an entity upon itself. When I capitalize the word, I'm referring to the industry and all that comprises it: the stations, the people, the business momentum it contributes to the economy, the programming it spews out for listeners and everything large and small that keeps it glued together and running. In any other context, though, I generally do not use caps.

By the way, I have also yet to settle on the correct way of spelling what I am. Americans use "deejay", "DJ", and "disc jockey" interchangeably. Internally, we often call ourselves "jocks". The Spanish say "disco jinete", the French use "disque jockey", and in German, you would say "scheibe jockey". Then there's the British.

In England and throughout most of the United Kingdom people on the radio are called "presenters". It figures people in a monarchy would find a way to make it sound like a class issue. The only thing more presumptuous than that is when deejays refer to themselves as "air personalities". But, in our defense, that was forced upon us. When radio sales departments began to print *"Account Executive"* on their business cards instead of *"Salesman"*, we had no other option but to upgrade our professional title from deejay to "air personality".

Call us what you like. We're the ones who roll into radio stations at 5 a.m. dressed in jeans and t-shirts, sit in our studios unshaven, and subsist on stale coffee and whatever is left in the vending machines. We're the ones who crack open microphones each morning and manage to connect it all into hundreds of radio shows that vibrate and pulsate through cities and open space alike.

Surely, if we did not have some divine purpose, why then would this Army of the Airwaves have a protector? The Patron Saint of disc jockeys is Gabriel the Archangel. Gabriel protects broadcasters, messengers, radio, and radio workers among others. Gabriel watches over us as we watch over you.

We play the tunes, ask the trivia questions, award the cash, make the jokes, keep the world smiling and sometimes even help it cry. If it weren't for us admonishing listeners to get their lazy asses out of bed each day, the country's productivity would surely be something less.

We're not the biggest cog in the economy, but we certainly help to keep it lubricated and considering how we get to spend our workdays…

…we just might be some of the luckiest sons-of-bitches in the whole world.

Chapter 2

When I entered Montclair State College (now a university), as an English major, my plan was to be a writer. That is, until one day when I was invited by an old high school friend to join him at the campus radio station and sit in on a music show he was doing. This was a revelation for me. I suddenly remembered what great fun it was to play at being a deejay and the thought of actually broadcasting was exhilarating. As he sat there and spun his favorite tunes, alternating between two oversized broadcast turntables, I thought to myself, "People make money doing this."

I never looked back.

I finished out my first year with new plans to transfer immediately to Kent State University, renown for its Telecommunications program and for students being shot by National Guardsmen during anti-war protests in 1970. Although I am fairly certain more people have enrolled for the former, not the latter.

Beginning my sophomore year, I began honing whatever broadcast skills I could. Of course, trying to learn about Radio through academia is like attempting to learn how to bungee jump by hooking your belt to a chandelier and jumping off your bed. There is no substitution for real life.

Kent had two campus radio operations: a closed circuit AM that was fed to the dormitories via the electrical wiring (yes, that actually works) and a bona fide, honest-to-goodness, genuine, transmitting-through-the-air FM public radio station. The AM played Top 40 hits and everybody in the Telecom program could have an air-shift if they wanted one, even if it was only 1 hour-a-week.

The Top 40 radio format was invented in 1952 by Todd Storz, co-owner of KOWH in Omaha, Nebraska and Bill Stewart, the station's Program Director. They noticed that customers in restaurants consistently played their favorite songs, repeatedly, on jukeboxes. Storz and Stewart simply transferred that concept to Radio, creating playlists featuring the most popular songs with instructions to play them more often. As Top 40 evolved, so did the DJs and many of them eventually became "pukers".

8

Pukers can only be described as DJs who spit forth a verbal presentation of words akin to some kind of spoken vomit that rises from the throat and passes by the larynx between each syllable. I wish I could be more specific. "Puking" is like porn: you know it when you hear it:

"It's Shunny and Sheventy Shix big degrees in the Capital Shitty on a *Shuper Shummer Shix Pack Weekend*!"

Almost all of us on WKSU-AM consciously chose to emulate the puker style.

Of course, pukers cannot fulfill their mission without jingles. This had long been ordained by *the* guru of all pop-music-programming-wannabes in the early days of Top 40. It came about when an unknown deejay went to the top of the Hollywood Hills in Los Angeles and heard the disembodied voice of Bill Drake - legendary AM programmer - declare, *"Thy Top 40 Radio Stations Shalt Have Singers Anointing Thy Station Names In Jingles."* And so it was and during the fourth Arbitron of the year, he rested.

At the time, there was *no* Radio *without* jingles. Therefore, WKSU-AM had no choice but to use jingles, too. Ours were actually jingles pilfered from demos of other commercial stations, which we butchered with an editing blade. We would extract bits and pieces from one jingle, then another until we brought to life some Frankenstein-like creation where the jingle singers sang a choppy rendition of" W-K-S-U". It was good enough for us.

Understand this was the Dark Age of Radio - the 1970s - when flimsy, brown magnetic recording tape spooled onto reels constituted the bulk of how programs and audio were distributed from one location to another. And if you needed to edit one of these reels, the only tool available to you was something called an "editing block" and a standard razor blade. You had to rock the reel-to-reel tape back-and-forth on a "tape deck" listening intently for just the right spot to surgically splice the tape. Then, you would carefully mark the cut with a white - sometimes black - "grease pencil" and spool the remaining tape further, looking for the proper place to rejoin both reels with a piece of "editing tape".

When I first learned how to edit, there were no digital software editors like the ones we have today. Back then, the term "undo" meant finding that piece of tape you cut out 10 minutes ago which you carelessly dropped on the floor. It was old school all the way. Editing was truly an art and to do it well, one needed a great ear and a lot of practice. However, do not be mistaken: it was inefficient and tedious compared to today's digital possibilities and I would never want to go back. Now, I can do sound production on my home computer with software equivalent to a 64 track-recording studio. There are Production Directors at radio stations who are so adept at digital recording their talent and creativity are stunning.

Frankly, it was thrilling to be on the air at WKSU-AM. I liked being in control, being the center of attention with the ability to claim responsibility - by name - for providing the "Hits" someone else was hearing. Sometimes, the phone would even ring and the sheer joy of confirmation, to know that someone really was listening, was just about the sweetest moment one could savor in the cramped AM broadcast booth at KSU.

I loved be a jock. It was fun and to me, prestigious.

I have never lost that feeling. Never. Each single day of my Radio career, I have continued to feel the glorious sensation of being special, of having been lucky enough to do what people in Radio do. It is why we broadcast and it is why we find it so hard to even consider walking away from it. Radio people are addicted to Radio. The hardcore ones will take a pay cut - if that's what it takes - just to stay in the business. We'll all put up with the bullshit and move across the country to stay in our field. Even those who leave Radio pine to come back, even if it's just a part-time weekend gig.

Radio is the heroin of the business world.

While WKSU-AM was light-hearted and easy-going, the FM side at WKSU was much more banal, anal and intense. The bulk of its programming was a load of PBS junk that was cycled from station-to-station on reel-to-reel tapes in what is now referred to as the prehistoric days before digital.

WKSU-FM did produce, on a local level, the obligatory classical music shows and even originated the type of eclectic programming you would normally expect from your nearby college station. You know: a couple of hours of music each week that could easily be mistaken for the sounds of screeching birds hitting the fronts of trains.

After some time doing grunt work on the FM side, I finally finagled my way into doing a morning wake-up show several times-a-week. By the way, let me now admit the only time I ever voluntarily changed my name for on-air was in college. On WKSU-FM, I was "Shane Harrison". I don't know why and I don't remember how I even came up with it. I just thought deejays were supposed to have fake names. For this transgression, I know I am still owed an ass whoopin' by the head of the Federal Communications Commission.

My dependability was noticed by the professor who ran the Telecom department and soon afterwards, I was awarded a coveted key to the production studios in return for certain tasks I agreed to be responsible for. This permitted me full access to the facilities anytime I wanted. Realizing I was not learning from my classes everything I thought I would need, I soon found myself spending countless hours, sometimes all night, tinkering in the WKSU studios on audio projects simply to learn how to edit, produce and create.

I never cared that much for the making of commercials or promos, which is what most Production Directors traditionally do. However, I was captivated by "long form" programming: documentaries, vignettes, and the like. Still, today, I think there is nothing more powerful than being able to tell an important story or an entertaining one, through only sound. When you do, your listener is an active participant and there is no more commanding communication.

I used my time well. In my junior year at Kent, I was hired part-time into the university's Office of Radio and TV Information. There, I was paid to produce public service announcements (PSAs) on behalf of the school along with a weekly public affairs program that aired on commercial radio stations around Ohio...usually at four in the morning.

Working in the Office of Radio TV Information gave me access to something which nobody else seemed too impressed about: all the recorded audio created by school and local radio reporters leading up to and during the days following the May 4, 1970 Kent State shootings, where the Ohio National Guard killed 4 students during an anti-war protest.

Prior to coming to Kent, I didn't know many details of those tragic days. However, my curiosity began to gnaw at me and I began to listen to the audio that was neatly labeled and stacked on the shelves. Maybe I suddenly cared more because I was a little older, a little more aware, or it could have just been because I had walked past the very spot where those students died, may times on my way to classes.

Call it perspective.

Nevertheless, the more audio I heard, the more I was affected by the passionate anti-war speeches by students and the comments from nervous National Guardsmen, who were not much older than the students they were pitted against. Each tape revealed another slow step toward the inevitable sound of gunshots and horror. It was then I realized this archive needed to be preserved in some fashion before it was lost or inadvertently discarded. In my searching, I could find no long-form historical audio record of the Kent State shootings.

Therefore, I began assembling the tapes and designating them chronologically according to the events. I read books on the shooting to insure I had the sequence correct. For weeks, during the summer between my junior and senior year, I spent sleepless nights in the WKSU production studios piecing together what I think is still, to this day, the most comprehensive audio account of what occurred on May 4. The final production ran about 80 minutes and it aired later that year on WKSU-FM and portions of it also aired on a radio station in New York City a year later. Shortly thereafter, the student council approved funds to press the production into vinyl for posterity.

My point: an event I was formerly detached from had suddenly become an impassioned obsession. Why? My perspective had changed.

Perspective and the good use thereof, is a tricky thing. Trying to develop a healthy perspective about you is like going out into the work world with a shallow resume. Nobody wants to hire you without experience and experience is nearly impossible to get without a job. It's the same with perspective: until you have something to look back on to analyze, you can't possibly learn how to avoid future pitfalls and mistakes. To put it bluntly: you have to step in some shit before you can figure out how to avoid stepping in more.

Luckily, life grants those without perspective one quality that helps to balance out this lack of wisdom, which only time can provide: blind, stupid ambition. It's a wonderful substitute for perspective because using it requires no justification nor does it ask for any rationalization. Blind, stupid ambition has little regard for failure and it generally comes in an almost endless supply right when you need it the most.

For instance, if I had listened to one particular instructor at Kent, I might not have ever tried being on the air. He thought I was terrible and gently encouraged me to pursue off-air facets of Radio. However, after some soul-searching, I decided he was just flat wrong. It's always good to keep in mind that some people, no matter how respectable they may appear, just might be full of shit. That's where blind, stupid ambition comes in handy. It let's you stand up for yourself when nobody else is willing. Don't be fooled. Trust your instincts because they will not deceive you. Recognize the "full-of-shit" factor. It pops up a lot in life.

One professor who definitely was not full of shit was Bill Randle, a legendary Cleveland deejay. By the time I got to Kent, Randle held a doctorate and was teaching Radio to wannabes like me. Randle was the epitome of a great mentor. He was a straight shooter who called it like it was. Of all the professors who ever taught me, he was the most honest about what Radio was really like. Maybe that's because he had seen it first hand during some wild times.

In an interview with singer Pat Boone by John W. Whitehead for an online journal called "Oldspeak", Boone said Randle, "was the nation's number one DJ at the time."

This was 1955.

"Whatever he said," Boone continued," and whatever pronouncement he made about a new record, that was it. All the other DJs around the country followed suit. That was before Alan Freed became so influential." (Alan Freed is the DJ credited with coining the term "Rock 'n' Roll" in 1955.)

Bill Randle had many claims to fame. Some sources insist it was Randle who discovered Elvis Presley. One fact is certain: he did introduce Presley on his first national U.S. television appearance, a program called "Stage Show". This was January 28, 1956 and what a great time it was for Randle, too. He was reaping the benefits of hosting both a popular show on WERE-AM, Cleveland and a weekly program on WCBS-AM, New York.

Bill Randle was no lightweight. In his day, he was a king maker of recording artists and is now considered a pioneer Rock 'n Roll deejay. If only all professors who taught Radio had such credentials.

After college, I returned to New Jersey. I thought I was going home. However, I was really only returning to shadows of what formerly was home. A month after I arrived, my parents sold my boyhood house, gave me $1,000 dollars from the sale, and moved to Florida. My folks always felt money could solve any problem, any situation, and any raw emotion. So, they threw some at me to makeup for bolting to Florida and although I felt a bit deserted, I wasn't mad. On the contrary, they had done more than their share for me. Their job was done. I took the money and found a one-room apartment in Bloomfield, the next town over from Clifton. The money kept my rent paid up for 6 months.

To survive, I immediately used my degree to land a prestigious job in the "fry" division at Burger King. From there, I became a bartender and bouncer at a biker bar. Let me point out that these two gigs might be the last documented instance of me contributing in some substantial way to the U.S. economy.

Although I tried, I was unsuccessful in finding any station willing to give me a shot on the air. Finally, I decided I would just start from a different direction. My first radio job was actually in sales at WPRJ-AM, a modest station in Parsippany, New Jersey. Even though I had grown up fifteen miles away, I had never even *heard* of Parsippany until I accepted the position. I was earning all of $120-a-week, which even then that was considered poverty level. The station was pieced together with a few old tape decks, just enough under-maintained cart machines to pump the audio through the console and something that resembled a transmitter.

I can't remember the deejay's names, but I know I was in awe of them because they were actually on the radio. I wasn't thrilled with selling commercials but at least I was inside a radio station instead of a fast food kitchen.

I quit a month later.

I know that doesn't sound very responsible but I was young and stupid - not necessarily always a bad thing. What sometimes may masquerade, as brash behavior can be, in fact, good instincts. Did you ever walk out on a job? Admit it: it felt good to tell people to shove it because as you slammed the door behind you, you were free again - and generally confident that you had done the right thing. You probably bragged to your friends about how you told the boss where to put it. They applauded you and you felt vindicated and cocky.

As we get older and more dependent on our increasingly larger salaries, we trade that freedom and confidence for a false security. This security is fictitious because when you work for somebody else, you *never* control the security you think your salary affords you. When you work for someone else, the more you make, the less security you have because it can be pulled out from under you at any time.

When you make less money, there is less to lose. It's easier to hold on to your principles and to appreciate your freedom - the freedom from having to answer to anyone but yourself.

In Radio, there is an old adage: *"You can't get ahead unless you get fired."* And believe me, Radio people are fired all the time. Sometimes it's for lousy ratings, sometimes it's because the station sucks and the format is going to change, sometimes it's because you're the scapegoat, and sometimes it's just because someone in management finally decided to can your ass because they figured out you make twice their salary and get to come to work dressed in a ball cap and shorts. And unshaven.

Being fired is an unpleasant fact. Therefore, the first thing you have to do is stop dreading it, no matter whether you work as a deejay, as a U-Haul rental agent (I've known my share), or at some odd little government agency that collects data on fish oil. Stop getting up everyday, looking in the mirror and worrying about what you can and cannot afford. What you cannot afford to do is to live in fear that your income will be torn away from you. How can you ever become a success if you are preoccupied with the possibility of imminent failure?

Imagine your worst possible scenario. Then, figure out how you would deal with it. Being in Radio, I have done this all my professional life because in a business as tenuous as this, chances are very good that worst possible scenarios will happen. Assume you lose your job tomorrow. Now what?

Bring in that perspective I mentioned before. There is only one big question you have to ask yourself, "Are you dead? Seriously. Are you dead? Because if you are dead, then you cannot fix anything and frankly, it does not matter if you are employed or not. Being dead is a *big* fucking problem in planning the rest of your life.

That, concisely, is my whole standard these days. That is the bar. That is what I measure every problem against because I assure you: no matter what your problem is today, chances are in one year - when you look back and you are past it - you will think to yourself it wasn't so bad after all. Granted, death was not always my whole standard. Admittedly, I arrived at it through experience and acquired perspective.

I'm just giving you a head start.

Weigh your problems against the vast concept of time and space. Did the Universe end as you know it the last time you failed at something? I doubt it. Did the galaxy suddenly blow up into a several billion pieces the last time you did not get a raise? Probably not. Did our Solar System vanish into a ball of exploding fire when you did not get a promotion? Nope. Did all of creation end when your last romantic relationship suddenly dissolved into a cesspool of hate and distrust as she threatened to slice you up into pieces small enough to fit into a box of Rice Chex? Okay, granted the last example is extreme and a restraining order might have been a good idea but I stand by my proposition: nothing blew up, the sun rose, the Universe continued to exist and you were left breathing in the end…in one piece and not inside a cereal box.

That's not a bad day considering the possibilities.

In 1999, 73 year-old Jesse Taylor of Windsor, Canada was dying. Ten months earlier, Jesse had been diagnosed with terminal lung cancer and, after unsuccessful chemotherapy, was admitted into a program, which was testing an experimental cancer-fighting vaccine. Jesse was hopeful the treatment might at least extend the time he had with his wife and two children. While being interviewed for a news story, Jesse remarked, "any day above ground is a good one." I'm not sure if Jesse coined the phrase, but he definitely lived by it.

My friend, life is an inexact science. It doesn't have nicely pressed edges and it is guaranteed to proceed in what will most likely appear to be random directions, unconcerned with *your* needs. Take heart: we're all sailing the same ship through these seas. Therefore, when the storm batters you so hard you think you are going to let go, let perspective work on your behalf because next to the big dirt nap, everything else seems somewhat less important.

Frank Sinatra once said, "You gotta' love livin', because dyin's a pain in the ass."

Amen.

Chapter 3

Once you adopt a reasonable way of viewing life and its ripples, it's important to try to understand the nature of how you commit to people and how others commit to you. Commitments, large and small, are what hold life together. You like steak? Lucky for you the cattle rancher gets his beef to market on time. You love your girlfriend? Lucky for you she promises not to sleep with the sailors on shore leave from the "U.S.S. Hornball". You don't like being charred beyond recognition? Lucky for all of us the U.S. government has treaties with other nations not to launch nukes.

A commitment can be many things: a character trait, the way you bind yourself emotionally to an idea or course of action, a written or oral pledge, a legal contract, and even the act of putting someone into confinement at a mental hospital. Those last two definitions are especially important because if you're in Radio, I guarantee you will one day look at a contract you signed and wonder why you should *not* be committed to a mental ward!

Luckily, I did not have a contract at my first job because I wanted to quit after the first 30 days and did. The next day, while moping around and wondering what in hell I was going to do for money, the phone rang. I was offered another sales job, this time in Plainfield, New Jersey at WERA-AM. Of course, I was not crazy about jumping right back into sales, but it was a slightly larger station - in another place I'd never heard of - and for more money: $150 dollars-a-week, a 20% raise from my last salary.

Best of all management said I could produce the commercials I sold. At the time, it seemed like the only way I was going to get my voice on a radio station. Understand, I needed the reinforcement of hearing myself on the radio to confirm I actually *worked* in Radio. No other evidence would suffice.

I worked at WERA for one year. Just so you know, in "radio-years" that's equal to about 3 years of regular, normal employment. That means if anyone ever walks up to you and says he was in Radio for 15 years, he deserves a gold watch with an inscription that says, "Thanks for your lifetime of service. See you on the links!"

Unfortunately, I never got off my salary draw, and was not terribly good at my job. I was too honest with merchants, especially if I thought their business would not benefit from the radio advertising. But, the job did afford me access to the studios after 5 p.m. where I endeavored to make a halfway decent demo tape of myself as a deejay.

The great lesson from this experience came from an unexpected place. Around the corner from the radio station, was a greasy little diner that made just about the greatest cheeseburgers I have ever eaten. Never under estimate the power of grease. Behind the counter where I usually sat, up against the wall near the cash register, was a small placard. It simply read, *"People Who Never Make Mistakes, Never Do Anything".*

Every time I ordered a cheeseburger, I saw those words and pondered them – probably dozens of times. The memory of this advice comforted me every time I did make a mistake for many years to come. Imagine that: absolution from a lunch counter.

After a year on the job, I realized I was not a salesman, would never be good at hawking thirty-second slivers of airtime and had taken a wrong turn in my career. Eventually, I began to hate selling so much, I would clock in at 8 a.m. and go to the park....or a movie...or somewhere until I could come back at 5 p.m. and clock out.

Finally, one morning I just walked in a resigned. I didn't have much money, was starting to slowly sink into an abyss of credit card debt, and since my folks were now comfortably settled in Florida I couldn't go home. I had no prospects, only a demo tape that didn't suck too badly. I left with it under my arm but was quickly distracted.

As it happens, while selling at WERA, I had befriended a guitar player named Shelly who was trying to form a band. He invited me to join it. Considering my Radio career wasn't going as well as expected, the idea of having a chance at music was very appealing. Shelly had great plans, knew a female singer, some other guy with a guitar and a friend of a friend who knew a music agent.

"Gee, how could we go wrong," I thought to myself as I skipped out on my apartment lease at 3 a.m. one morning.

Breaking rental leases is an essential skill for being in Radio. I should write a book on just that. And even though with this move I was technically going from Radio to music, never underestimate the usefulness in being able to disappear without a trace.

There are so many details you have to remember like *not* having your mail forwarded. Sorry, but if you want to stay one-step ahead of the rental manager you'll just have to give up any magazine subscriptions, personal correspondence, and – oh yeah - those overdue bills. Don't get me wrong: I really endeavored to keep my slate clean when it came to debts. But, I have no doubt I missed a few and over time and at some point there must have been creditors chasing me from one state to another over God knows what kind of balances due I must have left in my dust.

Another tip: if you plan to be in Radio, do not own a compact or sports car. More often than not, you will find yourself trying to fit everything you own into every corner of your car aside from the passenger's seat.

So, in the middle of the night I began to transport my belongings down two flights of stairs and made for the parking lot.

With that, I aimed my car east and moved into a communal house in Weehawken, New Jersey with Shelly and some other musicians. We knew we couldn't fail because, after all, the guy living upstairs from us had an actual talent development contract with a record company. We were convinced that meant something – a good omen - I mean, living near him and all, right?

You gotta' love blind, stupid ambition.

Weehawken became famous when Aaron Burr shot Alexander Hamilton in a duel on its cliffs which are situated across from New York City on the Jersey side, overlooking the Hudson River. On a clear day, you can look directly across the river and see West 42nd Street. According to the story, during a New York gubernatorial campaign, Hamilton dissed Burr who then got pretty pissed and challenged ten-dollar-bill-boy to a duel. So, on July 11, 1804, these two guys faced off not very far from where I now lived. Burr mortally wounded Hamilton.

On the day of the duel, Hamilton most likely had not considered the musings of the previous chapter concerning "worst possible scenarios". Hamilton's plight demonstrates my principle in the starkest of terms. If winning at life each day amounts to being left breathing, his pledge to defend his honor was a very bad decision. Had he taken my words to heart, Hamilton could have most likely bought his way out of it with a dozen donuts and a Double Mocha Latte from Starbucks. Judging from Burr's picture, he was a carb freak.

History be damned: there I was, living within earshot of Hamilton's biggest mistake. Little did I know it would turn out to be one of mine, too. But, I always wanted to try to make a living as a musician. So, I followed the advice of that little sign in the Plainfield diner that warned if I never made any mistakes then I probably could never say I had done anything.

I was broke in a year with no recording contract in sight.

The low point came when the band was booked into some crappy club that turned out to be a gay bar. In the middle of some acoustic number I was thinking to myself, "I am singing a love song to a man. Many men. This can't be good."

I started sending out that demo tape the next day.

I remember sitting in my room the night I came to my senses, strumming my 12-string guitar and refocusing my life. Being in a band was fun for a while, but it was time to get to work. Luckily, when I was twenty-two, I was still under the impression that being in Radio was "work". All of a sudden, I really felt grown up, especially being surrounded by a bunch of stoner musicians. This, no doubt, kept me motivated long enough to weather the next couple of months while I waited for the phone to ring with the offer of my next job.

A call came from a little station in Pennsylvania. Could I drive out for an interview? Sure! So, I jumped in my car and headed to Lewisburg, a quaint little town famous for its federal penitentiary.

Now, there's something a community can hang its hat on! I'm sure the Chamber of Commerce wrestled long and hard over which town motto to adopt to invite tourism:

"Escape To Lewisburg!" (rim shot)

"Lewisburg: More Pros Than Cons!" (rim shot)

"Lewisburg: We'll Keep You Captive!" (rim shot)

"Lewisburg: The Most Bars In Pennsylvania" (rim shot)

"Lewisburg: Have A Soap-Droppin', Bubba-Lovin' Good Time"

Thank you very much. I'm appearing at the Airport Holiday Inn all this week.

From this point you should know I will be purposely omitting some names of people and referring to them generically as the "General Manager" or the "Program Director" or "That Son-Of-A-Bitch Scum-Sucking Bastard", etc. No, it's not that my memory is fried, it's just that I may have occasion to say something not necessarily complimentary and to avoid embarrassing anyone - even though they may deserve to be publicly flogged with a copy of Rush Limbaugh's tax return, I have elected to omit a name rather than make up some fake one.

I drove five hours until I arrived in Lewisburg for my interview. Upon entering the General Manager's office I extended my right hand to shake his and suddenly realized he had no arm to shake back with. I immediately knew my interview was not going well. How was I to know the guy was missing twenty percent of his body? I mean, what could I say? "Wow! I bet that really helps you save on suntan lotion..."

It turned out he was not only the General Manager but also the owner. He proceeded to tell me about his quirky new AM station at 1010 on the dial called WTGC. The call letters stood for "Town, Gown and Country Radio". He went on to explain the "Town" was for the city of Lewisburg, the "Gown" stood for the local college community, Bucknell University, and the "Country" represented the rural areas. He was damn pleased with himself. He fully expected the station could appeal to everyone. Flat damn near everyone! All it had to do was play a little bit of music for every age group and every lifestyle.

I believe in this modern era of Radio, you would call that the *suicide* format.

Today, most Radio consultants would have him checked into a psychiatric hospital for observation. But, one can't help respect that kind of optimism. I admired his gumption. I guess one-armed guys develop a third testicle as a defense mechanism.

I had come out to Pennsylvania looking for an on-air position but what he really needed was a Sales Manager. So, we cut a deal: I would be his Sales Manager (as if I knew what the fuck that entailed) if I could also do the morning show. I would have agreed to just about anything to get on the air, and he must have seen me coming. He accepted my proposition. Let's see: General Manager gets to hire a guy for practically nothing *and* gets him to do second job before beginning first job of the day! Not a bad deal for him. But, what did I care? I figured I could live with selling radio if I at least got to be on it.

There was one more thing. He promised me that no matter how long I worked there, whatever sales I racked up, I would get my commissions even after I left. Are you sensing some sort of commitment was being made here? I could move to Goddamn Beijing and yes, I would absolutely, positively get my sales commissions. Swear to God. Really. On his mother's or my mother's or somebody else's mother's grave. Trust him! Cross his heart and hope to die (no, not with *that* arm, the other one. The good one).

So, I did. I trusted him. We made a verbal agreement. An oral agreement. A gentleman's agreement. It was the first one I made with someone in Radio and it was also the first one somebody went back on.

Gentlemen's agreements are no longer much good because there really aren't too many gentlemen around anymore - even if you shake on them and well, in my case that was not possible. Well, it was fifty percent possible. I imagine after Burr shot Hamilton in the nuts, most people figured being a gentleman was excessively dangerous.

The moral? If it's important enough to negotiate over, it's important enough to write down.

When you are in the heat of putting a deal together - for a job, buying a used car or deciding a pre-nuptial agreement - the other party is always going to try and make you feel like they are the nicest people God ever placed on this earth. So nice, in fact, that you can trust them to do the right thing. "Why quibble over minor details," they will say. "Why ruin this nice friendly chat over sordid little nasties nobody really cares about," they will say.

Bullshit.

If you are talking about promises, commitments, expectations or procedures that will affect you, your salary or your relationship with the other person or party, then it is perfectly acceptable to ask that everything you both agree on be written down and signed by both parties. Many times, earlier in my career, I did not insist on that. Why? Maybe I was not as confident in myself as I should have been. Maybe I was afraid the other party would get mad at my inability not to trust them. More than likely I just really needed the job and didn't want to make waves. Whatever the reason was, I was wrong not to insist on the finality of ink. I made this mistake over and over throughout my career.

It wasn't until much later did I learn sometimes even having it in writing wasn't good enough.

Enter the lawyers.

I once had to hire an attorney because my employer was a bitter old Scrooge who subsequently decided to be vindictive. All of a sudden, he informed me that my two week vacation clause really only called for one week per year. I know that seems ridiculous but you would be surprised at how precise wording needs to be in a legal document.

Section 10, Article 4 of the U.S. Constitution guarantees that, "...the right to contract shall not be denied..." So, don't feel like somebody hasn't already stood up for you on this matter. Plenty of our founding fathers yelled back-and-forth at one another when they ironed out this stuff a long time ago. You should take advantage of their good intentions. Never forget that John Hancock, the first signer of the *Declaration of Independence*, demonstrated quite clearly he meant what he said when he wrote his signature larger than any other signer, knowing that his actions would mark him as treasonous to King George III.

Large or small, a signature is still a signature.

Hancock was just trying to piss him off. You gotta' respect that.

Even if you don't have balls the size of Hancock (gee, how often does one get to pen a sentence with both "balls" and Hancock" in it without being employed by the porn industry), you, too, should hold fast for what you believe in and say and expect others to as well.

Offer your signature to seal a deal. Ask for theirs in return. Anything less is a disservice to yourself - and a warning.

Oh, and those commissions I was promised by the one-armed guy on various people's graves?

Never saw a dime.

Chapter 4

Having realized my big foray into the music business was less than glamorous or financially rewarding, I accepted the radio position in Lewisburg and moved to Pennsylvania as fast as I could. I rolled into nearby Sunbury where I took up temporary residency in the Sunbury Hotel, a quaint repository for transient people located in an attractively preserved old-fashioned downtown. It was fall, 1976, and even though America was celebrating its Bicentennial, Sunbury had managed to stay quite small, quite undisturbed, and quite manageable for most of those 200 years.

This was the big city to the local farmers and the closest place to Lewisburg I could find a cheap room. On Saturdays, the area farmers would drive into the town square and display their vegetables from out the backs of their pickup trucks. This was a real "Farmer's Market", not the kind cities put together after they've completed some fancy downtown redevelopment project in the hopes of luring tourists.

When I first arrived, I walked up and down Market Street to survey the area. Sunbury was barely more than a leftover collection of dated retail shops that continued to function solely because nothing bigger had come along to threaten their existence.

I grew up 10 miles west of New York City and by age 13 was regularly catching the DeCamp #66 bus into downtown Manhattan to catch a glimpse of the hippies and artists in Greenwich Village. I considered myself "big-city" savvy and to me, this was the sticks.

But, I knew why I was there. I was going to be on the radio. That part I was actually doing for free. My real job, selling airtime, would earn me a $145-dollars-a-week draw against commissions. But, as long as I had enough to pay my rent, buy gas, and feed myself I was fine. Money was irrelevant. My only concern was with one thing: what I was. And what I was - finally - was a deejay.

Since that one fateful day during my first year of college when I accidentally stumbled upon my future career at the campus radio station, I had been trying to breathe life into a self-image I had manufactured for myself. Most of us envisage who we are until one day we actually reach the point when we can assuredly announce to the world that we have become that which we envisioned. Me? There was a deejay inside who was trying to get out and this was the most promising chance I had been offered to date. I was going to be on the radio and this was payment in itself.

I lived in the Sunbury Hotel for my first 30 days in Pennsylvania, adapting to a drafty bathroom, stubborn shower, noisy toilet, and uncomfortable bed. Then, I moved into a cheap "apartment" that had actually been honed out of a barn on somebody's property in Northumberland, across the Susquehanna River from Sunbury.

Actually, there were two "apartments" in this barn. Mine was upstairs. It was a two-room living area that could have doubled as a refrigerator. It was October, a pretty cold time in Pennsylvania, and every time I stepped out of the shower, I froze my ass off. Ironically, it was the only time in my life I could leave a mess without worrying about my mother saying, "What do you think? That you live in a barn?"

Yeah. I did.

WTGC-AM was a newly established radio station. There were only a handful of employees. The one I remember most was an engineer/deejay named Dan. Dan had cleanly trimmed dark-hair, stood about 6 foot, was thin, probably 38 to 40 years old, and seemed to emit a mixture of quiet sadness and timid mystery. His wife had walked out on him and Dan had come to Lewisburg to "start a new life". He didn't like to talk much about her, but I suspect his oddness sent her running for the door.

I'm not a shrink but if you asked for my diagnosis, I'd say obsessive compulsive. The kind of guy who would put on a button-down white, cotton shirt and actually button the collar. Nobody I knew buttoned the collar. He looked out-of-place. He wore very thin, black belts on very unfashionable pants.

It was hard to believe this guy was a disc jockey. At the time most deejays looked more like Wolfman Jack sprouting long hair, beards, and carrying Alcohol Anonymous membership cards. Dan looked like an accountant. I got the impression his wife had forced him out of Radio at some point because she did not approve of it. When she left him, he probably jumped right back in.

As I said, there was a certain sadness to Dan which was unmistakable. You just knew he was crushed by his wife running out on him. Sometimes, he would talk about the great plan he had. He was going to become successful again and then, maybe, he would be able to put his marriage back together. She'd see. But, I knew that was never going to happen. He probably sensed it as well. It's like those people who commit suicide in the misguided illusion that someone will pay for it dearly. They think to themselves, "They'll see...when I'm gone...they'll be sorry".

They generally never are.

Radio is full of former and future successes. It's that middle ground - when you're neither - that's especially difficult. I have known talented guys who were trying to resurrect their careers because of a divorce, a drinking problem, bad ratings, and even jail time. I've also known people who were on top of the world, had the great gig, the big bucks, the trophy wife and the world by the balls. Deejays are either on their way up or on their way down. But, Dan was in the middle - in Radio Purgatory - and most likely, was destined to bottom out.

But, he had his plan just the same and I think if he didn't try to believe it might come true, he would have probably would have been sucking on the barrel of a pistol by the next song. Dan said WTGC was his last chance.

I believed him.

But, I could also see that Dan was more of a ghost than a man. Whatever feelings had once been inside him died after his wife left. You got the impression you could knock on him and you'd hear an echo.

The image of his face haunts me even today.

To look into it was to see despondency, failure, and sadness. Like Scrooge, who cowered when the *Spirit of Christmas Future* beckoned him to gaze upon his own gravestone, I didn't want to look too long into Dan's face because I sensed I might see what was in store for me, too. I used to wonder if someday I'd be stumbling around in a small, unfamiliar town trying to find my second chance.

Radio is full of people who are either so talented no other profession will coddle them as much as they require, so weird they can't function in a normal business environment, or so lonely their emptiness pushes them from job to job, searching.

Radio transmitter towers are like a beacon for an ever-traveling carnival of people who crisscross the country looking for admittance and acceptance.

"Give me your odd, your lonely, your weird - the ones out on bail".

But, even with Dan's presence haunting the building, I enjoyed working in Lewisburg because I was finally doing radio every weekday. Actually, I think Saturdays, too. The station didn't really have a Program Director so I played what I wanted, as long as the music stayed within the "Town, Gown and Country" guidelines that were set up by the one-armed guy who owned the place. I'm sure my air work was less than spectacular but it gave me a chance to practice, which is what I needed. Plus, everyday was a new opportunity to record myself in search of a better aircheck.

After the show, I would spend a good portion of the day trying to sell airtime. The spot rates couldn't have been more than 4 or 5 dollars for a 60-second commercial, if that. I still pretty much sucked as a salesman but surprisingly, this having been my third try at it, I did manage to sell enough spots to keep myself employed and on the air.

I only lived and worked in the area for three months. It was pretty lonely there. And every time I looked at Dan, his eyes looked so vacant I felt like if I got too close, I might just fall into him and never be found again. With my schedule, it was very difficult to have much of a social life. Plus, I was very shy and not very good at it meeting people.

What a sad irony: the person on the radio has listeners who think of him as a friend but, in reality, he has the least friends of all.

The person on the radio appears popular and glamorous but the reality is his life is probably more mundane than anyone's is.

This was I so many times. Many people in Radio are searching for acceptance on a personal level yet, being on the radio only reminds them how detached they really are; sequestered in a small studio, separated from listeners and barely connected by endless miles of radio waves.

I was restless. I kept thinking my life might be better if I just went back to Ohio.

So, I took a weekend trip to Columbus to see my old college friend Charlie. I never knew anyone like this guy. Charlie had balls as tough as titanium. There is no other way to describe him. He was also one of the best salesmen I have ever met. He could put his arm around you, lay out a plan, and next thing you knew, you'd be following him down whatever path he wanted to lead you.

He would have made a great cult leader. You would gladly drink his Kool-Aid.

Charlie was a smiling, frizzy-haired huckster who you couldn't help but like. After college, he set himself up in some sort of shady travel business. He would acquire travel discounts from somebody, somewhere and then resell them at a discount. It all seemed a bit queer to me. He appeared to be very successful, but I'm not sure how much of that was hype.

Anyway, I told him I wasn't very happy in Pennsylvania. He suggested I come and work for him. I said "Maybe" and he said, "Try it" and I said, "I'll think about it" and he said, "Do that".

We visited over that weekend and then on Sunday, I filled up at a gas station and drove out of Columbus back to Lewisburg. I was a couple of hours past the Pennsylvania state line and almost home, when I realized I needed gas. I pulled off the interstate into a truck stop and when I reached for my wallet....

NOTHING.

I frantically searched my car. No, it was GONE. I didn't know where it was.

Panic set in.

I tried to think. Then, I realized the last time I had seen it was when I topped of the tank in Columbus. I had to get back to Columbus. But, I had no gas and couldn't go anywhere.

In desperation, I got on my CB Radio and put out a distress call. Somebody replied. I explained my stupid, pathetic story. He said he would help. He would lend me the money. He wanted to know where I was. I told him.

When I think back now, I cringe. Meeting a stranger in a parking lot off the interstate late at night? He could have turned out to be a criminal, a thief, a murderer, someone looking for sex. Yet, I had no other choice but to trust him.

Twenty-five minutes later, I rendezvoused with this man and sure enough, he gave me $10 dollars and his mailing address. I thanked him and promised I would send him the money when I got back home.

I jumped back in the car and started back for Columbus. I got there sometime around midnight and went to the gas station where I had filled up. It was closed.

"Son of a bitch," I cursed over and over again.

I still didn't even know if my wallet was there or not. I had been driving all day and half the night, was hungry and tired and now I was way too far away from Lewisburg to get back in time for my morning air shift.

"Fuck," I thought to myself.

Now I had to call my boss and tell him I wouldn't be in for work.

"Yes, that's right Columbus - uh huh my wallet. Yeah, of course I like my job. Uh huh, no I swear I'll be in Tuesday. Yeah, okay thanks bye."

CLICK.

"Fuck," I again thought to myself.

I had committed the first cardinal sin in Radio: not showing up for my shift. Part of the trade-off for having a job where you don't work is the unstated understanding that since you've been given the gift of doing nothing for a living while still being paid for it, the least you can do is show the fuck up.

Today, if a jock can't show up, almost any station has the capability of shifting into autopilot because of computer automation and voice tracking. When I was starting out, that luxury was not usually open to station owners and Program Directors. No sick days, no personal days, no menstruation excuses because, baby - this was show biz and the show had to go on. Your presence was expected unless you were dead.

Part of that thinking hinges on the fact that Radio people bring something unique to an air-shift, mainly them. Our individual personalities, how we sound on the air, our idiosyncrasies, and whatever else it is we do is somehow responsible for people listening.

This is especially true of high-profile morning programs and talk shows. You can substitute one deejay in a music format for another and get by for a while but not so with the others. And all that money management pays you for not working? This is why. It's only when you can't show up for work that everyone realizes your value - and demands it.

The loan is called in, the bank threatens foreclosure, and the Godfather insists on repayment of that "favor" which was granted.

I figured I would probably lose my job having now demonstrated my unreliability. I went to Charlie's place and crashed. The next morning I awoke and went directly to the gas station.

"I'm looking for my wallet," I anxiously told the guy behind the counter.

"I think I left it here yesterday."

A look appeared on his face like, "Well it's about time you got back here" and yes, he assured me, I had left it on the counter when I paid for my gas. He turned away from me for a moment, reached down and retrieved it from where it had been safely kept. There was my prize: two credit cards, my license and whatever cash I had been carrying.

Ever since that day, it seems I continued to chase money from one city to another in the form of new radio jobs, new opportunities, bigger expectations and bigger paychecks.

Connect the dots between the cities I worked in and you'd have the trail of incarceration I consented to. Certainly I've reaped benefits and can't complain about my lifestyle. But, for this prize, I traded most of my freedom. I was at the mercy of whoever would hire me and wherever they were located. I lived in places I did not like and worked for people I liked even less. But, I made the money, cashed the paycheck and displayed the prize.

Maybe, sometimes the prize isn't worth winning if all it does is keep you hostage to the process.

In the beginning, the process itself was the reward. Being on the air and enjoying that wonderful feeling was the reason. Then slowly, I lost sight of that because ambition intervened. I wonder how many people have ruined their careers because of ambition. You start off doing something for a living because you love it and years later, you're cursing it.

My time in Pennsylvania was short-lived. I loved the air work but the loneliness was killing me. One day I just walked into the station and told the owner I was finished. Of course, he was "very understanding but a little disappointed".

I went back to the barn where I had been living and quietly packed up my things. I left behind a lot of stuff I had been dragging around with me. If it couldn't fit in my car, we would just have to part company. I

31

begrudgingly stacked the rejected belongings in the closet, figuring it might go toward the rent I owed on the lease I was skipping out on.

Sometime around 3 a.m., I vacated my barn, slipped out of Northumberland and absconded from Pennsylvania under the cover of night. I might have left a short note apologizing for leaving so abruptly. But, with a few months left on my lease, I was sure the only way out of this was to run. Mind you, this was no easy task. The barn was within sight of my landlord's house. I knew if I escaped, I would forever be a wanted man in Pennsylvania. It was a chance I had to take.

To this day, whenever I have to drive through the Quaker state, I break out in a cold sweat worrying that a State Trooper will pull me over for speeding and it will finally come up on his screen: "Skipped lease in 1976. Hold for questioning. Ask him if he wants his camping stuff back."

My tires spun past the Pennsylvania border at sunrise. As I entered Ohio, I again was faced with the daunting question of survival. I had about $200 dollars in my pocket and all my worldly possessions were in the back seat. Surprisingly, though, I felt confident and almost somewhat noble. I wasn't going to starve and I was free to go wherever I pleased.

I could still walk out of any job at any time because I didn't need any man's money.

I had a good feeling things were going to work out.

Chapter 5

I told Charlie I was going to stay for just a week or two. All I needed was some time to mentally regroup and launch my next career offensive.

"No problem," he said.

I was offered the room upstairs to the left of the staircase. It was currently being used as a rather disheveled storage area. I moved in.

Before leaving for Ohio, I edited the best-recorded air-check I had acquired from my morning show at WTGC. I found a map of the state and with a compass drew a 30-mile radius around Columbus. Then, I borrowed a copy of the *Broadcasting Yearbook* and looked up the addresses of any station in any town that looked halfway decent. I sent tapes and resumes to each one.

A couple of days after arriving, I received a call from a small Top 40 station in Chillicothe, Ohio, 1350 WCHI-AM, and was offered some part-time air work. I didn't know a thing about Chillicothe except that it was about 20 miles south of Circleville, known for holding a huge pumpkin festival each year because apparently, they had the best Goddamn pumpkins in the world there! The most pumpkins! The pumpkiest pumpkins! They ate pumpkins! They fried 'em! They boiled 'em! They baked 'em! They wore them! They built homes out of pumpkins! They apparently traded pumpkins on the New York Stock Exchange! They had even figured out ways to use pumpkins as deadly weaponry! Munitions plants covertly experimented with "dirty" pumpkin nukes that fit into a suitcase. You can't imagine the horror of infecting seven square blocks of an urban area with pumpkin seeds and orange gooey shit. Yes, I would now have the honor of driving past Circleville, Ohio, the fucking pumpkin capital of the free world and the most direct route to Chillicothe - which on its own was not known for a damned thing.

Things were definitely turning around for me.

I was hired to run the radio station on Sundays. All day Sunday. It was a "daytimer" which meant according to its license, it could not sign-on any sooner than sunrise and was required to sign-off at sunset. For some reason, the F.C.C., long ago, decided that there could be a whole shitload of real teeny-weeny AM stations all around the country that could operate on behalf of the local community, but only for part of the day. Then, like Cinderella ready to turn into a pumpkin (there's that fucking word again), they had to shut down and let the big 50,000 watt AM stations dominate the airwaves without the possible interference of these little bastard children. Isn't it ironic that the little stations that could serve the community better were the ones least allowed?

The first thing I had to do when I got to the station for my all-day shift was turn on the transmitter, which at that time required possessing what was known as a "Third Class Radiotelephone Operators Permit" with a broadcast endorsement. You legitimately had to know a certain level of knowledge about transmitters, electronics and broadcasting law to get one. It was so important, you were even required to take a written test at your nearest F.C.C. field office and pass it. Today, the rule has changed somewhat. There is no more test.

Today, a rhesus monkey can have a form filled out and mailed in on his behalf and within a few weeks, he, too, will be able to legally operate the transmitter at a radio station. Unfortunately, this hypothetical situation could actually never be tested since most rhesus monkeys have already chosen careers in management.

So, I turned on the transmitter. Then, I played back an hour or two of pre-recorded religious programming on reel-to-reel tape. The tape deck which these ran from was a fairly old, mechanically driven machine. No digital here. There were actually small knobs you twisted and turned to play the tape, rewind it, etc. On this particular tape deck, though, the "play" knob had broken off and all that was left was a circular metal shaft. The owner who hired me instructed me to simply use the nearby wrench and twist the shaft in lieu of a knob play a tape. What a fucking dump.

Somewhere around mid-morning, the doorbell rang and a preacher accompanied by a young woman with a guitar strolled in ready for their live show. The owner had specifically instructed me that I was absolutely not to put them on the air unless the preacher paid up-front. I sheepishly collected the check and showed them to their studio. At the designated time, I segued from the tape-recorded programming and opened his microphone. He introduced himself and began 30 minutes of a good old-fashioned fire-and-brimstone gospel preachin' that culminated in a musical hymn sung by the young lady.

After their performance and an obligatory request for donations from listeners, both bid me good day. I turned off the mike, played a recorded top-of-the-hour I.D. and put on a record. After seeing them out, I returned to the studio and spent the next two hours actually being a deejay. Sure, this was a real hole-in-the-wall with wrenches for knobs and pay-as-you-go preachers but I'll say one thing: WCHI had great jingles!

Never under estimate the power of great jingles.

I grew up listening to legendary Top 40 stations like WABC-AM and WMCA-AM in New York City and WWDJ-AM in New Jersey. They had great jingles. When I was in college, I listened to giants like WGAR-AM and WGCL-FM in Cleveland, Ohio. They all had one consistent element: great jingles. So, to me, great jingles confirmed I was really in Radio. I cannot lie: one of the happiest days of my life was when a radio station actually purchased jingles with my name sung in them!

At around 12:30 p.m., I had to join a network feed and pick up some sort of sporting event, probably a football game. I "rode" the board for a few hours inserting local commercials and doing live station identifications. After the game was done, it was back to the records until sunset. Then, to keep things legal, I played my last song, reached over to my left, and turned off the transmitter's filaments at exactly sunset according to a posted chart.

Day was done, gone the sun.

An orange glow resonated on the horizon. Or was it a reflection of those fucking pumpkins in Circleville? I don't know and it doesn't matter.

I worked there just one day.

That's because the next day, I received a call from the General Manager of WCLT-FM, a small station in Newark, Ohio.

"I'd like to talk to you", he said.

I drove out of Columbus and headed east for about 30 miles until I arrived at an exit that took me onto Route 13. I went north and as my car climbed a moderately steep hill, an old-style Radio tower with large feet made of sprawling girders appeared planted quite squarely on the crest ahead of me. I made a right turn into the parking lot and pulled into a vacant space.

Walking into WLCT-AM and FM was like unearthing a time capsule.

First of all, you don't usually find radio stations actually located next to their radio towers anymore. Most Radio stations today have studio miles away from their transmitter. They just relay their audio programming through a microwave or DSL telephone line. In my opinion, the physical separation of studio from tower takes a little of the excitement out of being on the air. I always have liked working right next to a radio tower because it's the tower itself that conveys the power of the medium.

Broadcast towers put a face on Radio, which normally functions as an invisible entity.

As you walked inside WCLT, you entered a large lobby. Reception was on the left, as was a hallway that led to offices and the current studios. But, if you walked to your right, you soon came upon a large, looming acoustically proper sound studio big enough for a band. The WCLT building had been built long ago during a time when radio stations actually had real bands providing music during live radio shows. To its testament, a piano still sat in the corner. You practically expected, at any moment, a pianist to sit back down and begin a cascade of notes to introduce the next act.

Thick, heavy curtains lined the walls which were designed to absorb and deaden any bouncing sound. Across from the piano, was the original control room, raised a few feet and visible by its sound-proof glass where producers, engineers and even sponsors had stood during live broadcasts decades earlier, observing programs in progress and congratulating themselves after a job well-done.

You could almost hear the voices embedded in her walls from years of regularly scheduled shows. I loved this place. And I use the pronoun "her", in the same way a captain lovingly refers to his ship or as a mountain climber pays homage to a great peak he knows deserves respect. Sometimes I would sit there by myself and imagine the radio shows still being presented. I could practically hear the words and songs that must have been broadcast. This old studio stood in tribute to the best times from Radio's past. I wish I had been there.

Another wonderfully quirky aspect of WCLT was the fact it not only had a real record library, but the original record librarian was still employed there and she continued to catalog and file new promotional recordings every day. I don't remember her name, but she was quite elderly and probably obsolete. Yet, the station would have never fired her. She had been there for so long management felt a responsibility to provide her with the job until she was ready to leave.

She did, in fact, retire shortly after I became employed, but was never replaced. Her position had become a luxury. However, this was during a time when "Mom and Pop" owned radio stations were more the norm than corporate radio and these individual owners had a defined sense of right and wrong. Employees really mattered a bit more. Radio mattered a bit more. People in Radio were more of a family because the uniqueness of what Radio creates on those airwaves had a binding tie all felt responsible for and all were appreciated for.

Let me tell you about this record library. It was literally a vault of golden memorabilia that could rival a museum's recording archives. The monetary value of the thousands of records neatly filed, categorized, numbered and shelved must have been staggering. This was the kind of collection you asked Sotheby's to auction off for you when you were ready to retire to an island in the Pacific.

You were easily looking at fifty years of recordings, from acetate disks of live war broadcasts to original Glenn Miller 78s in mint condition to original Elvis Presley discs on the Sun Records label. Name the artist, name the title and you could probably find it. Comedy, musicals, rock, country & western (what country used to be called), spoken word, and every other possible sound recording a radio station might receive in the mail or from a record rep. 45s, 78s, 33s, plain sleeves, colored sleeves, picture sleeves, the works.

Robert Pricer was the man who interviewed and hired me. He was the General Manager of both the AM and FM. Although everyone was permitted to call him Bob, I always called him Mr. Pricer. He was a typically bald, middle-aged, slightly rounded man who you would expect to be running a small-town radio station. Mr. Pricer had been there quite some time, having worked his way up to the best office in the building. At the conclusion of my interview he offered me my very first full-time on-air position in Radio.

I bid Charlie farewell and moved to Newark that week. I never had to drive through Circleville to Chillicothe again, although I'm sure - even to this day - the pumpkins pine for me late at night.

Initially, I did the afternoon show on WCLT-AM. It was a great job. I was finally working full-time in Radio and I didn't have to sell airtime to do it. I played records, read promos, PSAs and even did the "Obituaries of the Air" twice each shift. Each time an obit was read, the station got a dollar. "Dollar a holler" is what we referred to them as when the mikes were off. It was a real moneymaker for the company.

Everyday, the local funeral homes would phone in their list of dead people. The news department would take the info, carefully write it down on a special dead guy form, and put them in the studio. We would diligently read each name of the dearly departed one-at-a-time from the stack of forms at three designated times daily, telling our audience who was dead, how old they were and at which home they could be viewed. God help you if you were late with it; the phones would light up right away. Listeners loved this stuff. It was the kind of information only a local radio station could provide and although, at the time I thought it was quite odd, I sometimes wish I could work again where being on the air was so simple and important.

When I worked in Newark, Radio was still a business where someone like me could do just about everything there was to do at a radio station. Small market stations were the real training grounds for the business. I'm not sure too many of those opportunities exist today because of syndication, satellite programming, voice-tracking and a general lack of opportunity. But, in my case, I still benefited from an industry not yet corrupted by reforms of rules which possibly have not been in the best interest of the public nor the business. When I wasn't on the air, I did production. I recorded commercials start to finish; I wrote them, voiced them, and edited them. To me, this was grand.

The Program Director was a likeable fellow name Bob Brooks. You could tell that Bob had made a very conscious decision to try to grow as old as possible right there in Newark. He had no magnificent ambitions that I could see. He liked the stability where he was. Brooks and Pricer had probably seen a lot of guys like me come through their station, looking for a chance to do a little bit of everything, looking for the experience that would help them step up. They knew I was basically a short-timer. But, they didn't mind because they also knew there was always another guy behind me, ready to step in at any time. They seemed to enjoy the process. They seemed to accept it as a responsibility, too.

Mr. Pricer sensed I didn't have a "pot to piss in". Maybe that's why when he hired me he offered to rent me a small efficiency in a 4-unit building he owned. At $100-a-month, the price was right and I accepted. It was pretty small but, considering I was only making $150-a-week, it fit right into my budget.

A couple of months later, Mr. Pricer approached me and wanted to know if I wanted to make an extra $25 dollars-a-week. All I had to do was host a two-hour big-band show on the FM side. Well, I didn't know jack shit about big band music but I also could not turn down the money.

"Of course," I told him. $25 dollars was a lot to me. A week later, I was cueing up recordings recorded by Glenn Miller, Tommy Dorsey, Doris Day, Benny Goodman and dozens of artists and performers I had never heard of. Every Tuesday night, from 8 to 10 P.M., I managed to bullshit my way through another program, reading liner notes off the albums in the hopes of convincing listeners I wasn't a total idiot.

It worked.

I was feeling pretty good about myself, gaining experience on both AM and FM. I adjusted fairly quickly to my new job and home. Six months into my one-year stint there, I was promoted to the morning show on WCLT-AM and given another modest raise. Believe me, I was very grateful. The morning program was a six day-a-week job. Monday through Friday, I had a newsman but, on Saturdays, it was up to me to put together my own newscasts. This was an interesting process.

I would get up early enough to be at the local police station by 4 a.m. Once there, I would request to see the police blotter from the night before and scan it for arrests and incidents that might make for good news copy. By hand, I wrote down anything that looked interesting, and then headed to the station to type up my local news. Understand these were archaic days. I had no Palm Pilot to digitally store the facts culled from the police log or a laptop to write up the news stories. I had a pencil, some paper and a typewriter.

Back at the station, I would combine it with some state and national feeds from the Associated Press teletype machine and for the duration of my show became a newsman at the top and bottom of each hour. This was the type of hands-on practice which made broadcasters out of deejays. It is one thing to read a news story on the radio and quite another to know how to research it, write it and then deliver it with credibility.

Word processor or not, it was this type of experience which kept me in love with Radio. It's a good feeling of accomplishment to know how to piece together a radio program from front to back; from the music and the chatter to the news stories and even the obituaries. This is what I miss most about my early days in Radio: the joy of the process. When you have a passion for something, the newness of it is not dissimilar to the elation one experiences during early youthful sexual encounters. Every moment of discovery leaves you a little more experienced, a little more satisfied. And when it's over, you glow with a knowledge you did not have before.

Maybe if I had chosen to stay in a small market, I would have continued to do the important kind of radio that small communities rely on. It's low pay but also low pressure, simpler and very gratifying. Instead, my ambition and ego took over and pushed me on to bigger markets to make more money. Many people in Radio are afflicted in the same way, except maybe those who work in Public Radio. That's a special calling, like the priesthood. They know they're going to give up sex and make only a modest income. Well, honestly: who wants to sleep with a guy who hosts a Lithuanian folk music show and has to shore up his paycheck with a yearly telethon?

I wasn't ready to make *that* commitment.

Instead, I chose to work in that part of the industry where your success becomes an inverse ratio to how much amorality you'll accept. In return for ratings that translate into money, just how far will you go on the air, what outrageous thing will you say, who will you almost slander, what cultural mores will you trash, and how much bad language can you get away with before getting fined.

When Radio was still a more personal profession, where stations were owned by individuals and small broadcast groups, there was more camaraderie. It was like playing on a team you loved and all you wanted to do was win so badly you could taste it. Your General Manager was more like a great coach and the goals were simple: enjoy coming to work, have fun, get ratings and win. The sales department always made money if you did that. More often than not, the people who owned your radio station had some real programming experience. They had been on the air themselves, knew what it was like to be in a studio, and knew the electricity of knowing you were sounding great.

But, that has changed.

The Radio industry has forced itself into a corner of splintered demographics as each station fights over its share of a slowly disappearing pie, like a pack of wolves tearing the flesh off the hind legs of a small animal. The advent of Internet streaming and satellite radio has not helped. Anyone who came up through the small markets as I did knows the truth in what I say.

I worked at WCLT-AM and FM for a year. I wasn't earning much so I accentuated my income by becoming a bus boy and occasional bartender at the Buxton Inn located in Granville about 15 minutes west of Newark.

The Buxton Inn is Ohio's oldest continuously operating inn to be located in its original building. The Buxton most noted for the three ghosts that haunt it. The original owner, Orrin Granger, founded the inn in 1812 and was first seen – as a dead man - in the late 1920s. Unbelievably, he was spotted late one night in the pantry eating the last piece of pie. It is reported the owner at the time, Fred Sweet, actually sat with the ghost and chatted about the Inn and its history.

The second spirit who roams the premises is Colonel Buxton, who owned the inn from 1865 until 1905 and after who the structure was subsequently named. I was once told he had been spotted several times by waiters occasionally and fleetingly dining with live diners during the dinner hour.

The third apparition at the Buxton Inn is "The Lady in Blue", believed to be the spirit of Ethel Houston Bounell who ran the inn from 1934 until she died in 1960. She is sometimes blamed for the footsteps that are heard throughout the inn when no one can be seen and windows and doors that are opened and closed by no other apparent force.

Only one time did I ever feel like I was in the attendance of something not of the living world. One evening while bartending in the basement-turned-bar at the Buxton, a chill went through my body and I instinctively knew it was more than just cold air. It made my hair stand on end. But, none of the phantoms at the Buxton had ever harmed anyone so we all accepted their presence – or maybe they accepted ours.

Although I loved my radio job, Newark, Ohio was another one of those lonely places where everybody had grown up there but me. Once again, I was in a small town where I knew nobody and the chances of fitting in were already stacked against me.

Seeing my social prospects were inadequate in Newark, on weekends I used to drive the 30 or so miles into Columbus to meet girls. When I think back on those weekends, I scare myself shitless. This was at a time when the conscience of the country was not as concerned about the drinking and driving issue. Or maybe I was just oblivious to it. My trips into Columbus were a recipe for personal disaster. It was very simple: take one 30 mile drive from Columbus back to Newark at 2 a.m., add 6 or 7 drinks, one highly-curved two-lane road and what do you get? An almost dead me.

It is really a miracle that I'm still alive. I'm embarrassed to admit, and I shirk to really count, how many times I drove home in what must have been an unsafe state. The only explanation I have as to why I'm not dead is simply that I must have known the road so well, I luckily traversed it without serious incident each time. God probably had a lot to do with it, too. But, I'm convinced, had a county sheriff or deputy stopped me on any weekend jaunt, I probably would have been in jail.

The stupid things we do because we're lonely.

Forgive me.

Near the end of my year in Newark, Mr. Pricer came to me one day and told me he had an opportunity that might interest me. It seems a friend of his at a Columbus radio station needed a good employee. Was I interested? Well, you can imagine my excitement. To me, Columbus was like the golden ring, the "Winner's Circle" of my Radio world. It was the 35th largest market in the country and to work there would be a huge step for me. Was I interested? Yes! Of course I was! I didn't even care what the job was!

I was puzzled, though, as to why Mr. Pricer would present this opportunity to me. It certainly meant he would have to hire someone else and Bob, the Program Director, would have to train yet another employee. This couldn't possibly be good business, I thought. What could be in it for them? Why would they help me move up at their expense?

At the time, I didn't really know. However, later I came to understand the answer. WCLT-AM and FM were small, local stations and Mr. Pricer was a nice, local businessman. But, as humble as his place was, he still understood - quite clearly - how important his little cog was to the Radio industry. And, as such, he had a stake in seeing me succeed because he wanted Radio to continue to succeed.

He knew his place in the circle.

He was part of the appointed guard.

He understood and accepted that his station may have been a small one but; his duty to keep the business fueled with talent was a much larger one.

This man loved Radio.

I found out a few years ago that Mr. Pricer died. If I had been allowed to speak at his funeral, my words would have been very simple:

"He hired me when I was broke and needed a job. He offered me a cheap place to live. He presented me with opportunities. He was kind to me. He never screwed me. And when he felt I was ready, he helped me move on. This was a decent man and he changed my life."

I have never forgotten him.

Chapter 6

WRFD-AM was a 5,000 watt, daytime AM station, technically licensed to Worthington, Ohio - a stately suburb to the north of Columbus. When I arrived there, in 1978, it was owned by the Ohio Farm Bureau. As such, certain things were done simply because the Farm Bureau had ordained they be done that way and it mattered not what anyone in management or programming thought.

For instance: farm reports. Every day, three times-a-day, all regular programming came to a blinding halt at 8:00 a.m., 12 Noon and 5:00 p.m. to present 15 minutes of farm news. Pig futures, grain prices, fertilizer tips; whatever the fuck it is that farmer's talk about when they're not cashing their government subsidy checks for *not* growing stuff. Of course, I have to bow with professional respect to any other profession besides Radio where people are paid for not working. Never less, the reports aired and there was nothing anyone could do about it. Of course, the companies that sold their chemicals to farmers bought a shitload of airtime in and around those features which made the Farm Bureau very happy.

The General Manager, Joe Bradshaw, was pleased to have this income for the station but something pleased him even more: respectable, adult-type "good" music, as he called it, which at the time translated into pop standards from Perry Como, Dean Martin, The Andrews Sisters, Lawrence Welk, Mitch Miller, Ella Fitzgerald, Herb Alpert, The Ray Coniff Singers and dozens more who found fame from the late 1940s through the mid 1960s.

The General Manager was a nice enough fellow but, personally I thought he was a little nuts. The story I heard was that he had left Radio to sell insurance for 10 years and then - all of a sudden - one day came back. I think the Farm Bureau had something to do with bringing him back. There was also another little nasty rumor which I never confirmed about a couple of drinks here and there. But, like I said: the guy was okay. He didn't really care what else came out of the radio station as long as the music he liked was played. This was a mixed blessing.

It wasn't Bradshaw who hired me, though. I was interviewed and brought on board by the Program Director, Jim Keyes. He was a lanky man and not terribly tall as I remember. I was of the opinion if he hadn't been born a human he would have most likely been created as a deer - standing on a road somewhere, staring into the oncoming headlights of a Ford truck. He was a very likeable fellow but one couldn't help but wonder how he came to be running this radio station. He couldn't control the farm reports. He couldn't control what music we played. The only thing he could control was hiring the air staff and support people related to programming. He hired me to be the station's Production Director, which I did dutifully, five days-a-week.

On Saturdays, I produced a show that was hosted by an old radio pro named Spook Beckman. Occasionally, I did a fill-in air-shift. Granted, taking this position was a move away from the full-time air work which had taken me so long to arrive at but, I was so convinced my fortunes were tied to larger cities, I was willing to accept that sacrifice - at least for now. I just knew there had to be more money waiting for me in Columbus than Newark. I also knew that Columbus was a stepping-stone to even bigger markets.

WRFD did *All News in the Morning* until 9 a.m. Then a smooth and agreeable deejay named Denny Nugent spun records until 2 p.m. Actually, he relinquished the 12 Noon hour to news and farm reports and then came back until 2 p.m. Bill Stewart followed him and until sign-off. Bill was a naturally gifted humorist and sharing the same sense of humor, we became fast friends.

Bill was the first person I worked with in Radio who was able to convincingly pull off character voices, bits, and skits quite flawlessly. Surprisingly, he was never completely assured of himself. I did not understand, then, how someone anchored by such talent could *not* intuitively know how good he was. Yet, this is the curse that besets many brilliant performers in this business.

Radio is a dichotomy of self-worth. Some deejays boldly throw around their bloated egos, while just as many quietly wonder in desperation if their last show was any good at all. You've heard of buyer's remorse? A lot of us have "performer's remorse". So many on-air performers need to be constantly coddled and told we're good at what we do because we are the most insecure of all.

I enjoyed my work at WRFD, mainly because I enjoyed being able to say that I worked in Columbus. A lot of it was about status for me and at that point in my career, I needed that confirmation.

A few months into my new job, fate erupted. On January 26, 1978, Ohio was pummeled by the worst winter storm in its history, "The Blizzard of '78". The snow began to fall before dawn that day. Around 9 a.m. Bill Stewart and I jumped into his car and started to drive around Columbus, feeding reports back to the station on a portable MARTI unit. (MARTI is a brand name for a short-distance, line-of-site two-way radio transmitter/receiver. This was in ancient times, 1978 B.C. - "Before Cell" phones.)

We reported from the road for a couple of hours until visibility became dangerous and the chances of becoming stranded escalated to an unsafe disadvantage. Back at the station, Bill invited me to sit in on his afternoon show. By the time his shift began, an odd mixture of child-like exhilaration over snowfall and adult-like anxiety quickly turned into the realization that an extraordinary event was slowly choking the city into a standstill.

All reports indicated we were going to be hit and hit hard.

WRFD was licensed by the F.C.C. to operate during daylight hours at 5,000 watts on 880 AM with a pre-sunrise designation. This meant it could sign on before sunrise according to some goofy schedule but it still had to sign off at sunset to protect the frequency it shared with several other stations especially WCBS-AM in New York City. Of course, by sunset on blizzard day, we had a full-blown, 12-alarm emergency going with stranded cars, no visibility and a complete statewide shutdown. A quick call was made to the F.C.C. in Washington for permission to extend our usual hours of operation during the crisis.

Permission was granted.

Bill and I continued his show past sunset. As a matter of fact, we stayed on the air for the next 24 hours straight. Practically everyone else had vacated the station earlier that day. Those who could get out did. Only a skeletal staff remained behind and we were it as far as air-personalities. The news department was still intact during the storm and

News Director John Greiner along with reporters Mike Beard, Barbara Thomson and Mark Baer provided a constant flow of information for 34 consecutive hours.

During the night, while the winds howled and the snow battered Ohio, we fielded phone calls from listeners who needed help or just wanted to talk. But, phone lines were quickly going down and electricity was getting scarce. People were scared. Even we were operating on auxiliary power.

Because of our wattage and frequency, our signal bounced clear across the country that evening as we became a vital link for Ohioans and a beacon of information for the rest of the country. Although there was no Internet to speak of then, we were the next best thing to "instant messaging". That night, we broadcast messages from road-stranded travelers to snowbound families, from neighbor to neighbor, from the police to the public. We reassured and informed. We were the glue that held things together at a time when infrastructure could not.

I suddenly knew, first hand, the awesome power of Radio as I had never known before. Our voices blanketing hundreds of square miles in an instant, yet the perception of our conversation as personal to each individual as if we were sitting with them in their home or ditched vehicle.

This would not be the last time I'd be caught between the wrath of nature and a responsibility to serve the public.

I would be a liar if I didn't confess the rush you get from directing this kind of power. Having a captive audience in a situation where you are almost hero-like is indescribable. You know you like it but you're not supposed to, especially when so much danger exists at the expense of the circumstances. So, you try to act as humble as possible. But, in reality you feel pretty fucking special. If you have a conscience, you wrestle with the dichotomy for a while. But, in the end you just sit back and enjoy it. You're just too weak not to let the drug take over.

"The Blizzard of '78" bore down hard for two days, closing everything across the state: schools, businesses, roads, services, you name it. Winds were measured at 70 mph. Gusts up to 111 mph tore across Lake Erie, smashing into the north shore of the Buckeye state. Drifts were reported up to 20 feet high and temperatures dropped into the low teens.

People died.

A few days later, S.C. Cashman, Vice President of Operations for Buckeye Media, Inc., the subsidiary of the Ohio Farm Bureau that ran our station wrote,

The sincerity and the concern of the on-the-air people came through in a most touching and credible way. The number of people who called and told how grateful they were for the service being rendered was a real thrill to me....I'm convinced the station prevented much suffering, helped keep up people's hopes and moral and without a doubt saved lives. Those responsible deserve some kind of medal.

Well, no medals were ever issued. But extraordinary events are often the catalyst for changes in Radio. The blizzard changed everyone a little bit and management decided to make some changes, as well. Denny Nugent was fired, Bill Stewart was moved to mornings, Spook Beckman was put on middays and I was promoted to afternoons. In Radio, crises often foretell changes. If I hadn't joined up with Bill, my new fortune probably would not have happened. I had a moment to shine and management liked what they heard.

I was back on the air full-time and having great fun at WRFD even though the station's format was dismal. The musical mix was so old sounding, someone eventually coined the term "UnRock" and we actually began using it on the air as a positioning statement. "UnRock your radio" our jingles would sing. It was obvious we were appealing to a listener base that clearly needed hearing aids and wheelchairs. I didn't care. Not only was I on the air five days-a-week but also even had a jingle with name in it.

My show was mostly music but watching Bill Stewart gave me the confidence to try to do some humor. Some of it was pre-recorded characters and features I purchased and interacted with. It could be a little tricky: you played back audio from a tape deck and said your lines over silent gaps left between the recorded sounds. If your timing wasn't right, you'd wind up stepping all over the recorded material.

One series of audio cuts was a "reporter" who "filed stories" on my show about the disappearance of Toledo, Ohio. As stupid as it sounds – I got press from it. More importantly, I started to experiment in ways that would help me evolve from DJ into radio personality.

WRFD was also the first station that let me do on-air interviews. Some of the more famous people of the time I grabbed included actress Betty White, Allen Ludden (host of the famous TV program "Password"), Country singer and sausage king Jimmy Dean, actress Brenda Vaccaro, and others. You may not recognize some of the names but whom one gets on a radio show is a function of several factors: Quality of Celebrity Access = Market Size + Station Format + Station Ratings + What Year It Is. You'll see more examples of this as you read further.

The changes brought on by the blizzard also bode well for Spook Beckman. It seems that storm pushed many things around besides snow. Spook was no longer hidden away on Saturday afternoons.

Let me take a moment to tell you about Spook Beckman. Spook was an original. At one time, he was the most popular radio personality in Columbus. When he was hot, he was untouchable. He was an old-time, friendly, do-anything-for-you guy and people listened to Spook Beckman. He had his moment. But, by the time I came to know him, he was on the way down. Way down. His talents had been relegated to a weekend air-shift where he played big-band tunes and easy listening hits from the '40s and '50s. The dazzle was over, the flash was gone.

He was a has-been in the most literal sense. Yet, he still had a small, loyal following of people who almost patriotically tuned him in each weekend. They would call and reminisce about the "old days". For two hours each Saturday, Spook did the kind of radio show that had made him a local celebrity.

Spook Beckman never sold out. His style was his own and he stayed true to himself. Spook was the first to help me understand that what I brought to the radio - what any of us did - had nothing to do with the format we were working in or the music we played.

"When the song ends, my door opens up," he told me. "Then I go out there and give them *me*. And I do that until the door shuts and another record plays."

In Spook's world, radio personalities existed only if they insisted on it. The rest, well, were just deejays. I liked the way he thought.

On Saturdays, before the lineup change brought on by the blizzard, I was Spook's engineer. I started the records, opened his mike, told him what commercials were coming up, answered his phones and basically kept everything together. As I came to know him, it became obvious to me he was coming to grips with a career slowly fading away. How difficult this must have been.

Times had changed and his style just wasn't what most stations were interested in, except WRFD. At the time, WRFD was an enigma of programming. Against conventional wisdom, Spook's ratings were slowly climbing on his weekend show. Then, when the blizzard hit, Jim Keyes had a programming epiphany and Spook was kicked back upstairs into that full-time slot he so desperately wanted again.

That's the trouble with Radio: once it's in your blood, it might as well be heroin that you're shooting up because you're a junkie for life. It's fun, it's egotistical, it's intoxicating. The vanity is real but the self-importance is generally an illusion. Once you've been in the spotlight, it's hard to fade quietly into the shadows. Spook so desperately wanted another fix and he got it.

Not only did the great blizzard make more room for Spook on WRFD but it also laid a new path for his career. From WRFD Beckman was offered afternoon drive at WCOL-AM. The station even built him a storefront studio on Broad St. in downtown Columbus. For the next several years he again dominated Columbus radio, at least in revenue. Each day he would do dozens of ad-libbed spots, with little or no notes. The man was a master at communicating and in the end Radio chose not to leave him behind.

That cannot be said for many others. Radio is a harsh master. It has no room for the weak and no tolerance for the inadequate. Most of us cling to stay in it and few of us are strong enough to walk away from it. Those who successfully leave, always pine to come back. But, for most of us, there really is no leaving - successfully.

That rough winter was memorable in another way. Shortly before the blizzard hit, I had met my future wife. I was awestruck by her. She was a beautiful, young woman with long brown hair and a radiant smile. At the time, she worked in the Governor's office and had the look of a sharply dressed businesswoman, although she was actually trained to be an educator. We met at a nightclub and began dating. Okay, it wasn't a nightclub, it was a disco. There! I said it! It's true: at one time I wore open shirts, gold chains and shoes with very tall heels! Forgive me father for I have dressed - badly. Despite this, I met a wonderful girl who would actually go out with someone like me. Her name was Christine, and the first time I saw her, I knew I was going to marry her.

Eleven months later, I did and after everything Radio has thrown at us, we are still married. Not a lot of people in this business can claim one marriage that has lasted.

A lot changed during that one year at WRFD. In March, there was insurrection. The General Manager was served with a memo by five of us, including my good friend Bill and the News Director, Jon, expressing a "no confidence" in our Program Director. We requested he be removed from his position. Massive resignations were threatened unless action was taken. The G.M. had little choice. Faced with a walkout by the core of his air-staff, our Program Director was reassigned.

I have a long memory and remember both the kindness and ruthlessness that has been directed toward me. I admire loyalty and faithfulness and even though he had hired me, I turned against him and wanted him fired. It was contrary to my principles and a difficult decision. But, in the end I, too, signed off on the memo asking for his removal. My allegiance was invalidated by our opinion of his incompetence. None of us could stand by anymore watching one bad decision after another.

Jim Keyes' failure to win our confidence was not so much his fault as it was the General Manager's. Before coming to WRFD, Keyes he had been a floor manager, producer and director at a local TV station for ten years. He also had an advertising background. Notice I haven't said anything about Radio experience? Bradshaw brought him on board and when the shit hit the fan, defended his original decision in the *Columbus Dispatch* by saying:

"To me broadcasting is broadcasting (regardless of whether it is TV or Radio). To me there's no real difference, except that one has a picture."

You have to be fucking kidding me.

Even with his reassignment, by late summer of that year we all sensed WRFD was simply headed for disaster. It was time to look around.

By year's end, Joe Bradshaw was gone, too. And so was I. The day after Christmas, 1978, my new wife and I packed up our townhouse apartment and drove to Biloxi, Mississippi.

I was the new Program Director and morning man at WLOX-AM, truly one of the biggest mistakes of my career.

Chapter 7

I was young when I married Chris and we were both still restless. Her position as an assistant at Ohio Governor Jim Rhode's office was less than fulfilling for her and I, too, had expressed my job dissatisfaction by participating in the ouster of WRFD's Program Director.

I began to look for a new job and in November, Chris and I married less than a year after we had met. Before leaving on our honeymoon to New Orleans, I received a call from the General Manager of WLOX-AM in Biloxi, Mississippi, the 138th radio market. His name was Pat Finnegan and he wanted to talk to me about a job. Chris and I agreed to interrupt our activities for a few hours to drive over to Biloxi.

Looking back, I can't imagine what we were thinking. Finnegan offered me another thousand or so dollars than what I was already earning to work twice as hard in a market 100 steps smaller. Sometimes the only explanation for why we do things is because we *can* and nobody tells us not to.

I can only attribute our desire to escape from both our jobs as the reason we agreed. I suppose we also said yes because at the time, our commitments were still negligible. We could afford to make mistakes like this. We were a little cocky and felt invincible. To a certain extent, maybe we were.

We didn't have much money so it wasn't as if we were jeopardizing any substantial type of lifestyle. We were not beholding to anyone but our dachshund and ourselves. We were still quite free to fall flat-on-our-faces. After all, that is the "American Way". Maybe I was recalling that little sign in the diner back in Plainfield, New Jersey.

"People Who Never Make Mistakes, Never Do Anything."

I obviously had not made my share yet.

I drove down to Biloxi ahead of Chris to secure an apartment. Once done, I left my car there and took a bus back to Columbus; truly the worst travel experience of my life. I think it took about 20 hours to get home and most of the time I sat next to some smelly degenerate who, for all I knew, might have been a serial killer. At least I had plenty of time to convince myself of that.

The bus was so uncomfortable, so seedy, so lowbrow, I promised myself I would never board another one again. Maybe the bus ride back was also so awful because I knew I had made a big career blunder. The moment - yes the moment - I drove into Biloxi to get that apartment, I knew it.

On my return, it looked like a pretty shitty place all of a sudden. I must have been very intoxicated by my new bride during our honeymoon. How else could I have failed to see what a dump this place really was? Mind you, this was the Biloxi that was left behind after Hurricane Camille decimated it in 1969 and before gambling came to the city some years later.

This Biloxi was still, in many respects, psychologically and physically crawling back from a Category 5 hurricane that killed 200 people in a path of death from Louisiana to Virginia. Some building structures still stood naked where walls had been literally blown off, revealing nothing but the steel girders underneath. At the time, Mississippi was literally still a state of little pink houses. It was poor, it was backwards, and it was struggling to find its path to prosperity that other states had long ago been down. It was running last in the socio-economic marathon.

But, it was too late. I had resigned from WRFD. I had accepted this position. My word was my word. I blocked out any doubts and convinced myself this was going to be just fine. A few days later, on December 26, Chris and I took down our Christmas tree, packed up her car and aimed it south. We rented a small apartment near Keesler Air Force Base, which lay directly under a jet descent route. Even though the air displacement from the engines would shake us several times each day, after a while we didn't even hear them coming in for a landing.

My first day on the air in Mississippi was January 1, 1979. WLOX-AM was an "Adult Contemporary" station supplemented by a fairly archaic automation system which consisted of three large mechanical carousels that held several hundred magnetic cartridges containing music, jingles and commercials. This system was the granddaddy of today's radio automation, way before digital. The only "hard drive" here was the one from my apartment to the station every morning.

As Program Director, I inherited the rag-tag automation plus an afternoon guy who was quite a prima donna. We didn't agree on much and he was fired not long after I arrived. In his place, I hired Wayne, a fellow who had moved back to Mississippi to be closer to family he had in Jackson. The early evenings were hosted by an indigenous jock that played disco and dance records. He wasn't very experienced, but at least he showed up for work.

This was my radio station.

Honestly, it was disheartening. The highlight of my workday was meeting my wife for lunch. She, on the other hand, was lucky enough to find an office job working for a group of men who still felt women were second-class citizens. Yeah, we had really hit the jackpot. I would say, between the both of us, we had pretty much landed on our feet - in one big pile of shit.

One of the first promotions the station did was its yearly "Fishing Derby" remote broadcast. This was ordained by station history and demanded by management. I broadcasted several hours for each of three consecutive days from the end of a pier, closely surrounded by progressively rotting fish, which became ranker by the hour. This was a big fucking deal to the fishermen who lived down there. As I stood there each day, I prayed an errant hook would pierce the side of my mouth and drag me out to sea and just end it all.

Local radio stations make good money by selling "remote" broadcasts to businesses and commercial events. Usually a station can pocket anywhere from several hundred to several thousand dollars, depending on the market size. The jock who actually does the broadcast will customarily receive a talent fee.

Remotes are unique to Radio. Newspapers can't set up in front of a Wal-Mart and design an ad on the spot that will be immediately published and distributed in the hopes of bringing customers in before 5 p.m. TV stations do have the capability of doing a remote but it's more time-consuming and expensive and besides: you would be hard-pressed to find a TV station willing to interrupt their programming schedule for a 3-hour live broadcast from a tattoo parlor.

But, radio stations will do remotes for practically any reason. And the shittier the station you work for, the more remotes you'll do and the stupider they will be because the Sales Manager will take a check from anyone for any reason. Usually, it doesn't even matter whether the business or event the remote is originating from is of any interest to the station's listeners. It's economics.

There are some who will argue that income is essential (true) and a good deejay can overcome even a difficult broadcast situation (true again). But, that doesn't mean most remotes aren't crap. If a radio station is going to do a remote from a business, it should keep two things in mind:

1) Only do so if the nature of the remote itself will not interfere negatively with the station's programming and...

2) Whatever it is the business is selling should really be of interest to the station's listeners.

Otherwise, the whole event is a disservice to all involved. There is nothing worse than being sent to a place to do a broadcast and nobody shows up to see you. It means one of three things. Either:

1) Nobody listens to your radio station or

2) Nobody listens to you or

3) Nobody gives a shit about the business you are broadcasting from.

I'm sure I have been in all three situations during the course of my career. And the worst part of a remote that fails is trying to explain to the business owner or manager why nobody showed up, especially after he plunked down $2000 bucks for the station to be there and still has to give you another $150 for the talent fee. Most people in Radio develop a litany of excuses which can be pulled out when things seem darkest, like a "hail Mary" play in a football game:

1) The weather was bad - people stayed home. (bullshit)

2) the weather was too good - people were out but doing other things. (bullshit)

3) We should have offered more giveaways and prizes to get people in here. (bullshit)

4) Don't worry: there will be a residual effect in a few days from people who heard the broadcast. ("Hall of Fame" bullshit)

And the very worst part of all is trying to get your talent fee. Many times it is left to the jock, to physically collect the money from the business owner that day. This is the most cowardly thing an Account Executive or radio station can do to a deejay because it's the poor jock who is on the firing line.

If the remote sucked and didn't live up to expectations, he's the one who is going to get shit for how lousy it was. He's going to take the blame because he is the face of the radio station. No doubt the Account Executive who sold the remote probably slithered off an hour ago. Trust me: it is not a good time to ask for a talent check.

Remotes are like hookers: they feel good for a while but in the end, you wind up paying too much for too little.

After the "Fishing Rodeo", the next 9 months in Biloxi didn't go much better. Somewhere around July, the hottest time of the year, the air-conditioner in our apartment died and we sweated for 30 days before the apartment manager fixed it. Then, this very same asshole fumigated our rental while we were out and while our dog was still in it. He almost killed the poor thing! We were incensed. Traumatic as this was, it was still the calm before the storm.

Actually, it was two storms: Hurricane David and Hurricane Frederick. Hurricane David was only a Category 1 storm. It hit the coast of Georgia on September 4, 1979 and although it had been packing winds of up to 150 miles when it tore through the Caribbean, its effect on Biloxi was negligible. It kicked up the waves and wind, but otherwise was fairly harmless. Hurricane Frederick, on the other hand, was different. Seven days later, "Freddy" was aiming at the coastline of Georgia and Mississippi, boasting 145 mph gusts.

When alerts were posted, my wife and I rushed back to our apartment. Our place was fairly close to the coastline and a direct hit would have meant much damage. We began to do what everyone does when a hurricane is coming. First, we protected our windows with diagonal swathes of masking tape so if the wind blew the panes out, the glass wouldn't shatter as much. Then, the better furniture was elevated, if possible, on top of the crappier furniture to avoid water damage should flooding occur. Anything of real value like jewelry, cameras, photos and the like were loaded into her car. When we were done, she grabbed the dog and headed inland to stay with friends.

I had to go back to the station and when I got there, was in for one of the biggest professional disappointment of my life. My staff had deserted me. They fled! Really! Either they were cowards or I was plain stupid to think we should ride the storm out. Maybe a little bit of both. It's true, they had been through hurricanes and I had not. All the same, I was furious. More than that, I felt betrayed. Maybe this was the karma coming back to me that I created when I chose not to support our Program Director at WRFD.

It didn't matter, now, because there was no time to dwell on it. We had to make preparations for the worst. I was left, alone, to handle the station and to disseminate information as best I could. I only had the help of one person, a guy named Dennis, the only real friend I made while living in Biloxi. He had no radio background but agreed to stay and help in whatever way he could. I was very grateful.

As night came and ticked by, the storm intensified. I had that same radio rush as during the Ohio blizzard. It's weird how impending danger can seduce you. It's like some kind of fetish sex for your emotions. You get a flutter in your stomach and every once-in-a-while it races through your whole body for just a moment. It's like a fear orgasm.

Hurricane Freddy made landfall at Mobile Bay on the Alabama coast with a storm surge of 12 feet. So strong was it, Meridian, Mississippi experienced hurricane force winds 140 miles inland. Five people died and $2.3 billion dollars in damage was done. At the crest of the storm's power, it smacked Biloxi with 100 mile-per-hour winds. I had never been through anything quite like this.

I was on the air most of the night, taking breaks occasionally to get some coffee, to rest or to listen to the storm. Between midnight and 1A.M., I decided to see first-hand what this hurricane looked and felt like. I pushed open the front door and clung to the side of the building. My face was immediately pushed in by the pummeling winds. The energy and power of a hurricane is awesome. Imagine, driving in a car at 100 miles-per-hour and then sticking half your body out the window. I pulled myself back along the jagged wall of the station and fell backward though the open door to safety.

Here's how *Radio & Records* later reported it:

Corey Deitz, Program Director at WLOX/Biloxi, told R&R that at one point, all 12 of the city's stations were forced off the air. WLOX's tower was knocked down, but the P/A outlet managed to continue broadcasting storm news via an emergency hotline connected to WTIX/New Orleans, having thoughtfully made this provision prior to the storm's arrival. According to Deitz, 50,000 people were forced to flee the Biloxi/Gulfport area. Deitz also reported that the storm blew out the area's electrical substations, and as he watched, "electricity arced up in green lightning like something out of 'War of the Worlds'."

The next day - when exactly I'm not sure - the winds dissipated and the clouds tore apart to reveal a beautiful, calm day. The irony of a hurricane is that what it leaves in its wake is quite stunning. Here was the bluest sky one could experience and the freshest smelling ocean air you could inhale. In contrast - on the ground - lay downed power lines, business signs, street lights, pieces of wood, portions of buildings, glass, trash and anything else you can imagine that had not been strong enough to stand up to the winds.

When the roads became passable, my wife and I went back to our apartment to face whatever damage had been dealt. We didn't know what to expect. Our anxiety turned to gratitude when we discovered our apartment building still standing and the gratitude turned to relief when we opened our door to find everything still intact.

After Biloxi returned to normal I received a letter from the Office of the Federal Coordinator, Disaster Field Office. It read in part:

After Frederic hit, WLOX-Radio rallied first with initial coverage of the emergency and then giving this office complete cooperation in getting out the word on the disaster declaration....WLOX-Radio, went above and beyond the call of duty...

I would not experience a hurricane for another six years.

After Hurricane Frederick, I never felt the same about the staff who left me when they were most needed or the station I had poured myself into as Program Director for almost a year. My disenchantment soured me on being in management. What a lousy job, indeed, and what an ungrateful one at that.

I would not be a Program Director again for another 18 years.

Two months later, I accepted a position at WOHO-AM in Toledo, as their new early evening air-personality.

I was thrilled to be going back to Ohio.

Chapter 8

I arrived in Toledo in late fall. It was exhilarating to be back in a northern climate where the air was chilled with the changing seasons and the leaves hosted deep tones of autumn. On my return, I finally realized for the first time how much of my life and psyche were now tied to the Midwest and to Ohio. I had attended college in Kent, had worked in Newark and Columbus, married a woman born in Cambridge, Ohio and now I was back.

It felt great.

I didn't feel this way about Ohio when I first moved there to attend college. On the contrary, coming from New Jersey - just outside the New York metropolitan area - I was pretty arrogant about my new surroundings. Cows, barns, farms, and Amish. Everything was so different. I did not readily let Ohio inside me. I fought against it. But, ultimately, by my senior year, I finally conceded it was a much finer place than the crowded, fast-paced, and anxiety-ridden New Jersey I had grown up in.

Where your home is, is not necessarily where you were born or where you live now. There's only one place you can really call home. Home is the place you can return to, repeatedly, without apology and without explanation. It is where you don't have to work hard at being comfortable. Home is the place where you hope they'll bring you back to when it's time to be buried. For me, Ohio became this place and it crystallized in Toledo.

I knew two things about Toledo: A college roommate of mine lived there and actor Jamie Farr from the one-time hit TV sitcom "M.A.S.H." was born there. Oh, and it was the 82nd market - at least I was back in the Top 100. Other than that, everything was new to me. The city stood behind a minor baseball team called the "Mud Hens", had a hot dog fetish based in some interesting ethnic roots and mostly seemed to be a place that wound up in the punch line of many jokes. I didn't care. I was home in Ohio.

As usual - and what would become a familiar pattern - I went ahead to find a new place to live. Chris hung behind and packed up the apartment in Biloxi. We were both still pretty pissed at the manager for almost gassing our dog to death with his Gestapo fumigator so we agreed she should do what any self-respecting Radio wife would do: skip out on the lease and run like hell. Yes, we became fugitives from Mississippi. Now I was wanted for lease skipping in two states. And just when we thought we were free and clear, a letter arrived at the station telling us in no uncertain terms what criminals we really were and if we didn't pay the remainder of our lease we were surely going to be sued and in the end we would pay or go to jail.

I didn't mind the jail part, but there was no way I was going back to Biloxi.

Unable to afford to pay the remainder of the lease or hire a lawyer to represent us, I did the next best thing. I found a thick book about the law and composed a masterfully crafted letter outlining the injustices done to us and our rights which had been trampled upon. It was a superb moment which, no doubt, will go down in the annals of bullshitting history. As unlikely as it would seem, it worked and we never again heard another word. Sometimes in life, you don't have to be right or wrong. You just have to yell loud enough.

1470, WOHO-AM was one of a few stations owned and operated by a man who was not only a savvy businessman but one who liked to have his fingers in everything from sales to programming and promotion. But, then, that was the prerogative of an owner-operator. This was a time well before the Radio deregulation that occurred in the mid 1990s that allowed companies to own many more stations in any given market. Prior to that, "Mom and Pop" radio stations were the norm and the norm wasn't that bad. These stations provided individuality to Radio which, in the end, was as unique as the communities they served.

WOHO was the first station I worked at where there was true camaraderie between the staff. Jay Scott and Craig Edwards did mornings. Mike Morin was on midday, Beau Elliott was afternoon drive and Johnny Zion did overnights. We were all about the same age and socialized often with our wives or girlfriends. I never felt we were competing against each other but rather, we were unified in competing against the other stations - the way it should be. I fear that genuine caring and respect for fellow professionals is not readily seen much anymore. In today's Radio climate, less jobs and multi-layered responsibilities translate into more competitiveness within companies and less time to nurture relationships outside of work.

I began my run in Toledo doing 6 p.m. to 11 p.m. The show was initially a typical music shift but, eventually evolved into a mix of tunes and interviews. I slowly was able to prove myself as an interviewer and was allowed to expand on that. Topics ranged from UFOs, psychics, and ghosts to whatever celebrity or author I could seize. I was doing "Art Bell" before it was fashionable. About a year into my new employment, the Program Director approached me and wanted to know how I felt about developing a dating show on Friday nights during my regular shift. He had heard of the success of a show in Cincinnati called *"Desperate & Dateless"*. We decided to try it and immediately we ripped the name off and made it our own. It succeeded quite well.

The format was simple: the first hour of the show, we "registered" people looking for dates. I would talk with each person for a few minutes, find out some personal info about them and let the other listeners take mental notes. Then, beginning in the second hour, and for the next two hours, folks would call in and ask to talk with someone who had registered. My producer would call them up, and I would put both phone callers together on the air and just eavesdrop on their conversation. If I had to, I'd jump in to kick start the conversation but otherwise, they were left to themselves. Reality programming? You bet - and the city loved it.

"Desperate & Dateless" put me on the map in Toledo. The ratings climbed and the local media was intrigued enough to give me some press. All this commotion apparently translated into dollar signs for the station and the decision was made to move me to afternoons. I guess they were thinking they could capitalize on my success better in a drive-time slot. This was a defining moment for me. For you see, they wanted me to do something I had never been asked to do before: sign a contract.

Contracts.

Boy, if I could do it all again, the first thing I would have done before I ever even played a single record on the air would have been to go to Law School. (Actually, I finally did some years later but not soon enough!) Signing a contract with a radio station may seem to be a good idea, especially in a business that is so volatile. But, no matter how good it looks, the little bastard seems to always sneak in some fine print.

Actually the fine print is the same font size as anything else printed in a contract. But, words and phrases – they can be just so damn ambiguous - or open to interpretation - or vague. When I was younger, I mistakenly thought most people were not out to screw me. I have since come to learn that people don't screw people, contracts do. My dealings with contracts have been like a bell-curve over the years. I went from being very dumb about them to hiring a lawyer who was very smart about them to once again being very dumb about them – probably because I didn't hire a lawyer.

The rule of thumb should be quite simple: if you're going to commit to something on paper, make damn sure you really know what the words mean and *how* they can be interpreted. Words are tricky and lawyers are very good at plying them for the benefit of whomever they represent. No company you ever work for will construct a contract that benefits you more than them. I promise you that. Before you sign an employment contract, if you can afford an attorney, hire one. If you can't afford a lawyer, hire one anyway and work out a payment schedule.

Shortly before I was asked to sign this new contract, I did have one offer that was especially appealing. A new Washington, D.C. radio station was about to sign on the air: WJOK-AM, the country's first all-comedy station. They offered me afternoons for about $25,000-a-year. Being that it was the 8th largest market, I was ready to jump. But, Chris was against it because the salary really *was* a joke for a market this size. She was adamant and insisted we would starve.

In my heart I knew she was right but I still really wanted the gig. Reluctantly, I passed on it as I watched a good friend of mine at WOHO, Mike Morin, accept a similar offer there. In the end, the path not taken proved to be the right choice because WJOK only lasted a few years and then it was tossed on the trash heap of radio formats. It wasn't until the late 1990s this format was again resurrected – but this time in the form of online Internet radio.

So, I turned my back on the nation's capitol and instead signed a three-year contract with WOHO which basically gave me some built-in raises. That's about all I got out of it. The company had the upper hand. In effect, I was their Radio bitch and here's how that played out.

One day, while doing my afternoon show on WOHO, I did some mildly amusing but stupid off-color joke about gays. Well, before you knew it, the station owner had me in his office and he was furious because I was just an awful scumbag telling shit like that on the air - and what would people think - and that's not our style - and what am I going to do with you? Well, I'm thinking to myself, "Gee, I have a contract, what can he do?"

After some consternation, he told me in no uncertain terms.

"I'm going to put you on our new FM station. You will play music - then you will announce the music you played," he said. "Then you will play more music - and again announce what you just played. You will read the liner cards - and you will keep your mouth shut. You have a nice voice but if you say one thing I don't like, a joke, a crack, whatever - you're fired."

Oh, that's what he could do.

I had to go to my room without dinner.

I was in professional "time out".

I had fallen from grace.

And within a week, I was working on a brand new FM station the company had just put on the air called WWWM-FM. We called it "3WM" and it took some real concentration to say that legal I.D.

"Double-you, Double-you, Double-you, Em, Toledo".

Now, that's a lot of damn "Double-yous" in a row. It's a deejay nightmare. And you couldn't say "dubba-you". It had to be "double-you".

I was busted in rank from air personality *past* DJ straight back to *announcer* in the length of a jingle - and I pretty much hated it. Now I was back to doing the same duties I first did at WKSU-FM at Kent State: saying the station I.D., reading liner cards, pushing buttons, and waiting for songs to end so I could push more buttons.

Prior to working in Toledo, I didn't know the difference between an air personality and a deejay. In the beginning, it was all the same to me and I thought everyone on the air was a DJ. Now that I had begun to evolve and the genie was out of the bottle, it was impossible to put it back in. But, don't misunderstand: there are great radio personalities and then there are great deejays. They are different and both worthy of professional respect. But, what they bring to an air-shift is often two different types of entertainment.

Announcers, on the other hands, are like supermodels: their whole purpose in life is not to think; just to look pretty – or in this case sound pleasant. No one expects anything from them other than a string of non-offensive words every once-in-a-while. Half the time, you don't even notice announcers. They are background noise.

Management had given me the opportunity to evolve and now, they didn't know what to do what they had created. So, they hid me away as an embarrassed and misguided parent hides a retarded child in the basement.

3WM was absolutely mindless. I did a five-hour shift, six days-a-week and was bored stupid. I couldn't figure out if my contract had helped me or hurt me. Sure, I was still employed but the problem was I was still employed.

For the first time, I realized what a piece of meat a contract could make you. The terms of my deal were so general and so vague; management could put me anywhere, doing anything, anytime they wanted. Of course it was my own fault. They dangled regular salary increases and security in front of me and I signed it - without a lawyer - putting my trust completely in the company because I was sure they had my best interests at heart.

I'll wait until you stop laughing.

The whole concept of signing a contract in Radio for security is inherently flawed. By definition, as a noun, a contract is a legally binding agreement between two or more persons. But, as a verb, contract has many meanings including:

- "Squeeze or press together" - as in my nuts in a vice you're turning
- "Be stricken by an illness, fall victim to an illness" - as in the disease I have that makes me think exchanging my services for your money is going to go flawlessly
- "Make smaller" - as in my freedom
- "Compress or concentrate" - as in your moral responsibilities as an employer

- "Reduce in scope while retaining essential elements" - limiting my options so you can use all of my talents.

Most contracts in Radio are useless. An employer promises to pay you for a service and in return, you agree to provide it. And what exactly is this service? It's pretty vague. Is it your voice? Your sense of humor? Your warmth? The way you conduct a radio show? And how exactly do you conduct a radio show? Write it down and explain in detail and have that for me in the morning, okay? Do you do it the same each day? Do you plan it? Do you make it up as you go along?

Well, maybe all of that - unless you're not feeling well - or you're angry about something - or you're distracted because your girlfriend just told you she's pregnant - or you're just not feeling funny or friendly or warm or whatever it is you fool people into thinking you are everyday. Let there be no doubt: some of it is acting because nobody can be that fucking consistent in his or her life.

So what kind of guarantee does the employer get? Nothing, really, except the satisfaction of knowing that you'll be in the studio 4 or 5 hours-a-day, 5 or 6 days-a-week. We're talking about personal services contracts and aside from physically strangling the employee or putting a gun to his head, just how exactly does an employer get those "services" out of his contractual employee?

Management can't exactly hang you upside down and shake it out of you. Although, I'm sure some General Managers have fantasized about that. But, management can't. Not unless the employee chooses to uphold his end of the promise. And if the air talent suddenly refuses, what does the contract mean? Nothing. In most cases the employer stops paying the guy and the guy goes away, assuming of course that when he goes away, he doesn't cross the street and work for the competition. That's why employers like "no-compete" clauses.

When I worked in Chicago (we're jumping into the future for a moment), the Program Director who hired me told me an amazing story about the morning show that had just recently left the radio station. Apparently, these guys had been wooed to the Windy City by a General Manager who just thought they were Gods. After one or two failed attempts, he finally pulled all the stops out and said, "Just tell me what you want. Anything." So, these guys, on a lark, wrote down a wish list which was so ridiculous and so ludicrous, they thought that was the last they would hear from the G.M. On the contrary. He met their every request, down to what kind of snacks would be stocked in the vending machine! The team - stunned - accepted the job and moved to Chicago.

Some time into their employment, their wives admitted being unhappy with the city and began to needle their husbands. They wanted out. The morning team had no choice but to ask to be let out of their contract. The General Manager refused, repeatedly. He wanted their act on his radio station and Goddamn it, they had a deal.

Both sides were at an impasse. Finally, the morning team decided to just stop doing their act. They announced the time, the temperature and then turned the mikes off and played a song. In effect, they regressed to being just announcers. Still nothing. The General Manager wouldn't budge. In desperation, the team began to show up and play cards on the air. Finally, after several more weeks of this nonsense, the General Manger relented and tore up the deal.

You cannot make people do what they just do not want to do.

And even though a contract cannot force a personality to perform, it can still imprison both employee and employer. I've been on both sides of that. In Toledo, my contract was my jailer when I was given on-air duties which I found boring, inane and unfulfilling. Later in my career, contracts I signed would work on my behalf, imprisoning employers inside agreements that could only be broken by paying me a lot of money to go away. I've been fired three times and have walked away each time with thousands and thousands of dollars under the agreement I would not work.

With the amount of money some radio stations waste, you'd think they would be more comfortable purchasing parts for the Pentagon.

Chapter 9

I don't remember how many months I announced the time and temperature, read liner cards and then said "WWWM-FM, Toledo". But, I do remember how angry I was. I felt like I was simply wasting away. What pissed me off the most was how subjective it all seemed. I crossed over somebody's "line" and everything I had accomplished up to that point was seemingly wiped clean by a faux pas.

Unfortunately, when you work for someone, it's always his or her line, not yours.

We can be a fairly unforgiving society and Radio is an unforgiving business. All it takes is one mistake, one gaffe, one off-the-cuff quip, and your career can spiral. The renowned radio host, Greaseman, knows this all too well. In 1999, he was fired from WARW-FM, Washington, D.C. for what was deemed a racist remark. The Grammys were to air that night and after he played a clip of a Lauryn Hill song he remarked, "No wonder people drag them behind trucks."

It was an unfortunate and callous reference to James Byrd, Jr., a black man who had been decapitated and killed while being dragged behind a pick-up truck in Jasper, Texas. Most likely, Greaseman probably regretted saying it the moment it left his lips. But, the damage was done. He was fired later that day. He held a press conference to try to minimize the damage but the injury was done and it took him several years to rehabilitate his career.

In 1981, Howard Stern was fired from WWDC-FM, Washington, D.C., when he called Florida Airlines to ask what the fare was for a one-way ticket from National Airport to the 14th Street Bridge. One day earlier, a Florida Airlines jet had crashed into that same bridge. It just takes one comment to take you from on the air to on the street, or as we call it in Radio, "on the beach".

Sometimes, radio personalities say things quite deliberately. Other times we say things in the heat of the moment which we probably would not have said in any other situation. When you're on the air, you're performing within the parameters of an on-air persona you have created and honed over years. This persona sometimes has an existence of its own and it is often oblivious to good sense.

But, when "it" fucks up, you take the hit. Of course, try telling the General Manager this explanation for why people are picketing outside your radio station calling for your resignation and he'll laugh his ass off as he signs your last paycheck.

In Radio, when you apply for a job, you send an "aircheck". An aircheck is usually an hour or two of your Radio show which has been "telescoped". Basically, the middles of songs and commercials are deleted so whoever is listening can concentrate on the person's performance within the context of the flow of programming. When you apply for a job, you send an aircheck - nowadays on a CD or as an .mp3 file via email - and the Program Director allegedly listens.

Essentially, your whole career - your life - your next meal - comes down to the best aircheck you can come up with and usually, when you need a great aircheck the most, you have just been fired and you probably haven't been airchecking lately. The best you can hope for is that you recorded yourself and stashed a few good ones away over the past couple of months. This is the radio equivalent of "backing up" your hard drive. Many radio people don't do it very conscientiously. Then, when their job suddenly "crashes", they run around in desperate search of decent audio. Unfortunately, there is no tech support for radio careers. So, if you're in the business or even plan to be, don't forget to back up your career on a regular basis!

Once your aircheck is selected from the queue piled on the Program Director's desk and actually listened to, he will most likely *not* take the time to hear the whole thing. The common rumor is you receive about 10 to 15 seconds to make an impression. I tend to believe this is true because having been a Program Director twice, that's all I ever gave somebody else's aircheck.

It's not that the Program Director is necessarily cruel. Rather, he's probably just busier than hell and has a fairly good idea of the sound he's looking for. So, first impressions count. You'll get no opportunity to convince him that you "grow" on people, even if you do. There will be no chance to state your case to explain how good you are at getting publicity or how much community involvement you are capable of or even why you are out of work...again.

You get 10 to 15 seconds. So, good luck, pal. If your voice is squeaky or weird or you don't have the kind of sound the P.D. thinks will blend with the station's image, you're gone immediately. If you get past the first 15 seconds and he hasn't tossed your CD in the trash or sent your .mp3 file into the "Deleted Items" folder, then maybe - just maybe - he'll listen to a few minutes and possibly the whole aircheck.

That's why you labor over your aircheck. You re-edit it, you equalize it, you snip it and cut it and take out all the lousy mistakes you can without it sounding like you took out all the lousy mistakes you could. You want it to sound perfect, yet natural. Of course, every Program Director knows that each aircheck has been edited to be perfect, yet natural sounding. So, since he has to assume every tape has been "doctored" up, in a way, they all wind up competing on the same footing.

Doctoring airchecks is the radio equivalent of athletes taking steroids. Yeah, you're not supposed to do it but boy, the results are great.

So, there I was sending out copies of my best aircheck looking for a new job, hopefully to get out of the music box I was imprisoned in. After some weeks of searching, I finally had an offer from WRVQ-FM in Richmond, Virginia to come and join their morning show.

All I had to do now was get out of my contract.

This was one of those moments where in reality, a contract was truly worthless. I no longer wanted to provide the services the company was willing to pay me for. They could stand on their heads until they turned blue in the face and I didn't want to play anymore.

I relished this moment. I savored the feeling of being on the verge of obtaining my freedom once again. There is nothing quite as exhilarating than having a secret like this. It feels great when you know you are going to inform someone he or she can no longer control you. You've quit a job before, haven't you? Maybe you walked out, impulsively - in a blaze of glory - because you had just had enough. Or maybe you had secretly sought new employment and waited until you could force the moment and take command.

Nothing says it all like, "Fuck you. I quit."

I walked into the General Manager's office and announced I wanted out (minus the "fuck you"). Of course, he didn't make it easy. There was immediate indignation. People don't like other people walking out on them whether it's a romantic relationship or a job. It pisses them off because suddenly you have taken control of the relationship and you are wielding the power. To management, especially, this is tantamount to an ego crisis of Biblical proportions.

The General Manager rambled on about how much time I had left on my deal and how much they liked having my voice on their little jack-in-the-box-music-service. Then it began to turn ugly; what an ungrateful person I was and how could I do this to them after all they had done for me. It was the typical management "Hail Mary" play: he threw everything he had at me for as long as he could. But, in the end, what choice did he have? He grudgingly conceded.

My release was also easier to obtain only because I intended to leave town. Had I wanted to stay and work at another station in Toledo, the company probably would have held me to the agreement.

Radio stations don't usually like their staff walking out. They hate it even more when on-air people want to leave to go to another station in town. Even if an air personality despises his present company so much he would spit down their throat, light up their broadcast tower with gasoline, and do a death dance in a loincloth in front of their billboard rather than one more air shift, some stations just will not let go.

I liken it to when you're driving down the highway behind some guy in the left-hand lane. You want to pass, but he won't move over. He figures, since he's doing the speed limit, what right do *you* have to go faster than he does? You're invading his space and damn it - he's not going to move! Instead, he's going to express his dissatisfaction and keep you "in line". He transforms into a "citizen cop", ready to enforce the law of the land on your ass. His immature actions temporarily control you and he feels powerful. Well, radio stations drive in the passing lane, go the speed limit and don't take kindly to their deejays speeding by.

Similarly, many stations don't like their jocks "passing them up" and moving ahead to another station in the same town. They perceive this will somehow damage them. Ironically, the real damage is letting the guy still work for the company, knowing he hates the situation as much as it appears. What company in their right mind wants to keep paying an employee they *know* not only can't stand working for them, but also hopes they go down in a flaming heap of charred cinders? Would Microsoft keep disgruntled software engineers around and never think they would plant bugs in the software and screw up the code? Wait a minute...that could explain why Windows sucks so much.

In the end, I was given a written release from my contract. Two weeks later I left my pregnant wife behind to manage our affairs and I set out for Richmond, Virginia.

During my years in commercial Radio, I have lived in a great many places.

Every time I have had to move, it required at least one and sometimes two temporary residences before I could bring my wife and later, children, to join me. Usually we were selling a house and Chris would hang behind until that was done. The Richmond move only put me a month ahead, which was a relatively short time, considering some later moves.

Driving into a new city is an anxious experience, especially for me, since I really have no sense of direction. And because I always have a short-term and long-term plan in my head about how my life is supposed to go, having no sense of direction defeats my mental mapping and stresses me out.

So, I grab onto any familiar path I can learn that will get me where I'm going and never waver from it. It doesn't matter how many shortcuts or alternates you show me, I will most likely stick to my original. Car bombs could be exploding on the street and insurgents could be shooting at my tires. Doesn't matter. I'm sticking to the way I know.

This drives my wife crazy because she *has* a sense of direction and cannot imagine why I insist on routes that might be a greater distance even though shorter ones exist. She fails to understand the security it gives a no-sense-of-direction-person to be able to get somewhere by themselves even if it takes twice as long.

Richmond is a quaint city blended together by a combination of newer high-rise buildings and older, traditional structures, some dating back to the turn of the century and earlier. When I arrived, it was the 53rd largest radio market in the country.

The fist thing I did was find the station's facilities located on Church Hill, a famous landmark. Only a few yards away from my new studio, on March 23, 1775, the great American patriot, Patrick Henry, entered what is now named St. John's Protestant Episcopal Church and uttered his most famous speech:

If we wish to be free ...we must fight! I repeat it, sir, we must fight! An appeal to arms and to the God of hosts is all that is left us! ...I know not what course others may take; but as for me, give me liberty or give me death!

How appropriate given my recent escape from Toledo.

Jeff Morgan, the Program Director greeted me and said arrangements had been made for me to temporarily stay at a motel near the airport. Oh God - another 30 days in the hole. I have attempted to add up the amount of time spent living in motels, hotels, and badly lit and cramped efficiency apartments and the sum equals years. It scares me how much time I have spent waiting to be settled. Luckily, I only lived by the airport for a month.

"Q94", as it was called, turned out to be wonderful and probably the best place I have ever worked. I accepted the job taking a decent raise in salary to join the morning show where I could once again, be more of a personality than just some buoy floating in a radio wave giving the time and temperature. If the air-staff in Toledo showed me what kind of camaraderie was possible within a radio station, the people at Q94 taught me what a Radio family could be like.

I was first hired by Jeff to join him on the air. At that time, the trend in Radio was quickly moving toward morning shows that featured more than one high-profile person. Initially, though, I think he really saw me as a sidekick and I was fine with that. The station was happy to have me and prior to my arrival, plastered the city with big maroon billboards which said in white lettering "WHONUQAMDJ?" (Who New Q AM DJ). The week I began on the air, one more line was added: "Corey Deitz 6 -10 a.m. Q94".

Damn if I didn't over-sleep my very first morning. The night before my debut, I was absolutely wired with anxiety. I couldn't close my eyes. I kept thinking whatever I did, I could not screw up my first day. Around 2 a.m. I passed out. The next thing I knew, the phone on the nightstand rang and the voice on the other end said, "Good morning sleepy head. It's 6 a.m." Well, I about died! An apology fell out of my mouth; I hung up, cursed myself for being so stupid and sped off to the station. Morgan thought it was pretty funny. He was an easy kind of guy.

Unfortunately, Jeff was fired about two or three months after I was hired. I don't exactly know why but rumors about it swirled through the offices and studios for weeks. Let's just say as a gentleman, it would be inappropriate for me to discuss certain alleged indiscretions.

Just as quickly as Morgan was terminated, I was catapulted into anchoring the morning show by myself. I realized this was probably a great opportunity, so I worked hard to do the best shows I could. I spent hours preparing material at home and even more time in the production studios, creating bits, skits and recorded material.

After about 6 weeks, Phil Goldman, the General Manager, announced that someone named Bob McNeil was going to be the new Program Director. I was pretty nervous about this, knowing how meticulous a P.D. can be, especially about people they have not hired themselves.

Let me first tell you just a little about Phil Goldman. Phil Goldman was one of the nicest men you could ever meet in this business. If I had to make a list of great people I've worked for, he would tie with Mr. Pricer from WCLT- AM/FM in Newark, Ohio. Phil Goldman was a slightly short and rounded easygoing Southern boy with dark hair and a wide face. He reminded me of the Cheshire cat from *Alice in Wonderland*.

Goldman may have seemed harmless on the surface, but below his friendly charm was a very shrewd and cunning man. If he was dealing on a business level, he would project this country-bumpkin persona and lull his business opponent into a false sense of security. All the while, underneath, the brilliant Phil was planning and scheming how best to get what he wanted out of whatever deal he was working on. This was his business gift.

He was like a Trojan horse that liked Chinese food.

Phil was notorious for walking through the halls of Q94 around lunchtime, grabbing anyone he saw and inviting them to have lunch with him - usually at his favorite Chinese restaurant. I never worked at a station where the boss asked you to pal around with him. It made me feel like I mattered. Phil was a generous man, a kind fellow and a straight shooter. If Phil gave you his word, you could trust him. He was a gentleman who could shake your hand and uphold his end of a gentleman's agreement. Quite rare, indeed in this business.

WRVQ-FM began its existence as WRVA-FM in 1948. At the time, the F.C.C. designated its power at 200,000 watts. In 1962, new power regulations were put into effect and the new limit for FM stations was lowered to 100,000 watts. Fortunately, the original "Superpower" FM stations were grandfathered by law and permitted to maintain their full strength.

Goldman put Q94 on the air in June of 1972. The station's name was changed to WRVQ, signaling a break from its traditional sister station, WRVA-AM. At that time, FM was a fledgling frequency and was still quietly making inroads. Goldman hired a young Program Director/DJ named Bob McNeil and the both of them created what would become a giant in Top 40 radio.

By the time I arrived at Q94 in 1983, it was legendary. To its credit, Q94 became a major stepping stone station. Consultants, on a regular basis, raided the air staff with job offers or recommendations to clients who were looking for Top 40 air talent.

So now, Phil had brought back Bob McNeil to once again, program the "Q". It must have been a tough negotiation because part of McNeil's compensation was the use of a Jaguar. Not bad. Soon after his arrival, Bob called me into his office and we talked for a bit. I thought I was going to be fired for sure. Actually, I have spent most of my career thinking I am going to be fired. I'm not paranoid - I'm pragmatic. Instead, he announced he would be joining me on the air. I didn't know what to think. Working with my boss on the air? How weird would that be?

Every mistake I made, he would see. How could this ever be comfortable?

As it turned out, it became a very successful relationship.

Many dynamics were at work and they converged into a monster. McNeil's intuition, a group of talented people he assembled and a new idea from Tampa, Florida ultimately propelled our show into being the most talked about, highest profile morning show Richmond and central Virginia had ever heard.

Something extraordinary occurred. We caught lightning in a bottle. For the first time in my career, I really was in the right place at the right time.

Chapter 10

Bob McNeil brought together a mix of people who he thought had just the right chemistry to pull off something new that looked promising. It was going to be called the "Q Morning Zoo" but eventually was also known as "The Q-Zoo", "The Morning Zoo", and even just "The Zoo". By the mid 1980s, when you said "The Zoo" in Richmond, everyone knew you *weren't* talking about the one with the animals.

Chances are, you've heard of or listened to a morning show sometime in your life where the word "Zoo" was part of the show's title. It all began in Florida. The flagship station for the most copied morning show format in Radio history was located at our company's Tampa station, WRBQ-FM, known locally as "Q-105" and owned by Edens Broadcasting.

Scott Shannon and Cleveland Wheeler were having great success with the original "Q-Zoo" which they created at WRBQ in 1981 and McNeil thought the idea was ripe for Richmond. We became the third station in the country to do a "Zoo" format. The Richmond "Q Morning Zoo" went on the air in April, 1983 just in time for the spring Arbitron rating period.

Actually, a rival station in town almost eclipsed Q94's decision to convert the morning show into a Zoo. At the time, WEZS-FM, an Adult/Contemporary station known as "EZ-104", was doing quite well. Their morning show was anchored by a two guys who called themselves *"The Love Brothers"*. Somehow their station got wind of our plans and suddenly they began throwing the word "Zoo" around during their morning show. We were livid and there was actually some - not much - but some discussion as to whether we should proceed with that name.

All EZ-104 knew was that we were going to use the Zoo moniker. They hoped to interfere, cause confusion and generally screw with us. That's the way it's done in Radio: covert ops are continually carried out. It's not just a job, it's an adventure. Finally, after some consternation, we all made the decision to introduce Richmond to the Q-Zoo a few days before originally intended.

It was the right decision. The Q Morning Zoo came on so strong EZ-104 quickly backed down. "The Love Brothers" hurriedly abandoned any "Zoo" references and made the decision to hunker down and stick with the brand name they had already taught the market to recognize. It was a short burp in Richmond radio history and the average listener probably never even knew it occurred. I think you would be hard-pressed to find someone, outside of our original circle, who would even remember this short but important skirmish for Zoo "rights" in Virginia.

As part of the new Q-Zoo, McNeil had hired an old friend of his, Rita Bentley. She joined the station with split duties. Off the air she assisted Bob in the programming department but on the air, she was *Betty Bodine*, a country-fied, trailer park queen with an every-woman mentality almost anyone could relate to on some level. She also created other memorable characters like *Susan B. Anthony Jones*, a humorous black character, and *Wanda Bondage*, a sex therapist. Rita's characters were so clever and funny, she later syndicated them to stations around the country.

Next, came Mike Rivers. Mike hadn't been out of the Navy for terribly long when he was offered employment at Q94. A more talented guy, you could never meet. His forte - to
almost an obsession - were funny characters and solid comedy writing. He was a brilliant performer but his pursuit of perfection sometimes was confounding and curious. Mike's most
popular character was a sports reporter named *Parker Field*, named after the local baseball diamond. Sometimes, Mike would come to work *as* Parker Field. And if you needed to talk to Mike about something you had to address him *as* Parker Field.

I liken it to the line Sigourney Weaver's character uttered in the movie, "Ghostbusters", when she became possessed by an arisen demon.
"There is no Dana, only Zuel."
Sometimes, there was no Mike, only Parker.

Mike was the ultimate method player, to a fault. He was also very inventive and created other personae like traffic reporter, *Radar Dodge* and the *Right Righteous and Reverent Harold Dean Sasser*. In the 1980s, every respectable Radio show had its own reverend.

Initially, the team was rounded out by Q94's longtime News Director, Treeda Smith. Later, her role on the show was assumed by John

Lawrence, who brought a hip, conversational, and lifestyle-oriented style to the news.

I anchored our Zoo. I was the nice guy, the balance, the guy who said, "Oh No...that would be wrong..." McNeil was the nut ball, lunatic, gadfly, troublemaker - a perfect role for him since, as Program Director, he didn't have to answer to anybody, except Phil Goldman. McNeil's genius as a performer was knowing when to push the edges and when to break through the old boundaries. He said and did things I never thought you could do on the radio. It was eye opening, to say the least.

Bob was also the first person to show me that it was okay *not* to be perfect on the air. That is to say, he didn't worry excessively if he stumbled over some words or forgot what he was going to do or what direction we were going to go in a break. He was real in the best sense. Working with McNeil was a liberating experience. My old notions of what somebody was supposed to sound like on the radio were peeled away and discarded forever.

Although I never told him, I idolized McNeil. He was only a few years older than I was, but his grasp of this medium and the audience was stunning. More importantly, he was a risk-taker, if it was a calculated one he thought he could win. Believe me: there is no success sweeter than the one you achieve by a risk other's think will be your demise.

McNeil was just arrogant and clever enough to lead us to that kind of victory.

Of course, at first none of us really knew what this Zoo was supposed to sound like, not exactly, anyway. We were feeling our way, like a blind man with his hand on a wall. In the beginning, Scott Shannon and Cleveland Wheeler sent us a few "Zoo starter kits" as we called them. They were tapes with bit ideas, skits, sound effects and other production elements from the Tampa show. For the first few months, we'd get a new tape every few weeks. Then, once-in-a-while we would get on the phone with Shannon and just talk about what their Zoo was doing and how we could better emulate their success.

The company flew me down to Tampa to sit in and observe Shannon and Wheeler doing their now legendary Zoo at WRBQ-FM. At the time, these guys were already the radio monarchy in Tampa. I tried to steal every good idea I could.

Within six months, we had a fairly good model in place. The show consisted of benchmarks like birthdays, trivia, horoscopes, and recurring characters like *Mr. Leonard* (a squeaky-voiced character ripped-off from the Tampa Zoo who was always "*sicker than a dog*"), Parker Field, and Betty Bodine. We spoofed everybody and everything using fake commercials, parody songs and original skits. Radio in the 1980s was all about pre-recorded bits and sound effects. We couldn't get enough of them. I had never done radio quite like this and I loved it. McNeil encouraged us to be creative and Goldman stood behind us every time we got in trouble.

And we did get in trouble.

The new Q Morning Zoo was such a radical departure from everything people had been used to hearing, it was considered scandalous. We took shots at politicians, celebrities, traditional mores, TV, movies, and even ourselves. You name it and we joked about it. The key to the Zoo format was the texture and layers this ensemble of people brought to the show. It was a radio buffet comprised of music, sound effects, voices, characters, information, jokes, skits and anything we could imagine trying.

At first, not everyone appreciated it. Within the first couple of weeks, some sponsors jumped ship. But, Phil Goldman never flinched. Bless his heart. This was the kind of guy you wanted to work for. Goldman had faith in the Zoo format. He had seen it succeed in Tampa and was of the mind to let the people he hired do their jobs.

Gary Edens, the patriarch of our parent company, Edens Broadcasting, wrote to me in April of 1983 and said, "The Q-Zoo in Richmond is going to be a smash hit."

He was right.

It paid off, and handsomely, too. The Q Morning ZOO became the hottest show in town and every single advertiser who ran from us in the beginning, eventually came back. We were vindicated.

I was once reminiscing with Rita Bentley about the early Zoo years and she summed it up quite well.

"We were like the Beatles", she said to me.

And she was right.

Once the show picked up momentum, we could do no wrong. When we made appearances, we were mobbed with listeners. The ratings skyrocketed. People recognized us in public. We were on TV, we were on the news, and we were in the papers.

We were famous in Richmond. But, not only there. With our station's 200,000 watts of power we soon discovered our following reached throughout Central Virginia. We could travel 60 miles out of town and a crowd would still be waiting to meet us. This is what every radio personality dreams of.

The Q-Zoo had its own look and culture, too. Bob and I made appearances dressed in safari outfits wearing green pith helmets. We had an ape for a mascot. Our logo featured a monkey and a banana. We ran jingles that sang "*Dazzle the Dorks*" and then lambasted local politicians, poked fun at pop culture and simply laughed and enjoyed ourselves four hours each weekday. We also spent a lot of time with charity events and community projects.

We were golden. It was like having the best day of your life 5 days each week.

Of course, as with any radio show with the right elements, the program got better as time went on. To say we found our niche would be an understatement. We created a new one. The Q-Zoo became a new standard for morning shows in Richmond.

Before I drag you forward and any further, some things must be stated for the record about Q94. The record must be clear about some very extraordinary people. The best deejay I have ever known will most likely never receive the recognition he deserves. His name is John Staton. John did nights and could talk up a song intro to the vocal perfectly, each time, every time, and anytime. He never screwed it up and he made it sound casual and flawless. He didn't bitch about needing "more time" to talk to "do his thing" because his "thing" *was* being a deejay. Unlike today, there was no voice tracking. Voice tracking let's the jock record his break and then fit it neatly between two songs. In a sense, that's cheating because it requires no skill, no timing, and no grasp of the rhythm that permeates a four-hour radio show.

With John Staton, it was live and real. You gave him the music, the promos, the prizes and the liners and he gave you non-stop, perfectly executed wall-to-wall deejaying. This can be an art and with him, it was. More importantly, John loved what he did.

Unfortunately, he had to leave his full-time gig at Q94 when his father passed away. John was needed by his family to continue the family business and he did the honorable thing. But, John Staton continued as a weekend deejay through the '80s, '90s and into the 2000s doing weekends at Q94. It never mattered to John that he had to drive about an hour-and-a-half each way to get to Richmond to do his air-shift. This is dedication. And love, too. This is the kind of radio person you want to hire, work with, put your trust in and count on.

Roger St. John was Q94's midday personality. He was a veteran jock, too. Roger may not have had the technical prowess of John Staton, but what he did possess was an enormously infectious personality and a shared love for just being on the radio. Roger knew it was a gift to be able to come to work each day doing such a fun job. He had no specific aspirations to be more than what he was because he was proud to be a disc jockey. This was the kind of guy who relished being on the air, enjoyed personal appearances and made anyone, any listener, feel at ease. Everyone loved Roger St. John.

Even though Q94 was the first station I worked at where I was more than just a deejay, John Staton and Roger St. John taught me how honorable being one could be. Contrary to what some might think, you can't put just anyone on the air and expect he will succeed. In the end, it takes a certain skill and a certain charm to create the connection between listener and performer. These guys had it.

John King, Robyn Bentley, Billy Duncan and Mike Gedding were some of the other people who all came together to create WRVQ-FM as I knew it in the mid 1980s. I think if you asked them, they would tell you that their experience there was probably one of their most memorable.

The Q Morning Zoo was inventive, humorous and also fairly edgy for its time. There was a lot of sexual innuendo and plenty of controversial chatter and opinion. Part of the reason it was so successful lay in its ability to use misdirection. Famous magicians through the years have used this tool to fool audiences. We used misdirection to push the boundaries. The concept is simple: if people like you they will not only let you get away with a lot, they'll even defend you when you go too far. For all the off-color humor, shots at people we took and sexually oriented bits we aired, there was always a balance of "good guy" stuff.

The Q-Zoo was the King of good guy stuff. We were always jumping on a local cause, raising money for a burn victim, having a food drive, and making an appearance at a charity event. We were "nice guys" and people appreciated that. Our community involvement and citizen service usually gave us a pass to go over the line. If we offended someone, it was usually neutralized by the person standing next to them ready to defend us with "...yeah...but think of all the good things they've done."

As an example: every week, Rita Bentley (as her character Betty Bodine) would visit children of listeners who were hospitalized. She, along with another character, "Granny Getwell" (played lovingly by my wife, Chris, in full "granny" costume) brought small trinkets and toys to sick children. Once a week, Rita would announce which hospitals the duo would be visiting and listeners would call to get their kids on the list. It was a brilliant public relations tool and positioned the Q-Zoo in the most positive light. Who cared if we insulted someone's sensibilities once-in-a-while? How could you *not* like a radio show that did things like this?

Unconditional love.

Yes, Phil Goldman put out plenty of fires we started but, in the end, the people knew we had good hearts. Today we are drowning in radio personalities who think the only way to get ratings is to be mean-spirited, nasty or by practically slandering someone else on the air. The truth is it's just as easy to be a nice guy as it is to be a dick. I'm not saying you have to be wimpy. On the contrary, if someone is a dope, call it like it is. The trick is to balance everything.

Q94 and the Q Morning Zoo was a monster. September 7, 1984, Joel Denver wrote in *Radio & Records*:

[Bob McNeil]...piloted Q94 to a commanding string of victories...since he rejoined the station a year ago. Not only is WRVQ number one overall, but it's the leading teen station by a sizable margin, and is also on top with 18-34, 18-49, 25-49 and 25-54 adults!

Then, about a year-and-a-half into the second *McNeil Era*, all of a sudden it looked like the bottom was going to fall out. One day, Rita came to me and said," Bob is leaving."

"What?" I responded.

"He's taking another job."

I was crushed. More than that, I was scared. I think I even felt betrayed. Bob was our mentor. He was the Svengali who had the vision to help us paint this wonderful radio portrait. What would we do without him? Could we have a "Zoo" without McNeil?

We were all quite depressed.

For a while, a lot of pressure fell on my shoulders while the station searched for a suitable replacement. When you are accustomed to performing in a two-man situation, the second person becomes a bit of a crutch. You know you can usually count on him or her to pick up the slack and catch you both if you start to fall. Each one is the other's safety net.

Eventually, the station decided on Garet Chester as the on-air replacement. Garet was a nice enough fellow who had most recently been the sidekick for another Richmond morning show at WRNL-AM, a country station. Garet's background was stand-up comedy. He did characters, some voices and had a fairly "common" sense of humor. I don't mean common in a negative sense. I mean he was in touch with the everyday people in town, something I probably didn't appreciate enough at the time.

Garet was from the Richmond area, whereas I was a transplant. He understood nuances I couldn't. Simply put, this was his backyard. By the time Garet and I had teamed up, I had become somewhat narrow-visioned in my approach to creating comedy for the show. As I look back, I appreciate his style more today probably because it is closer to what my own eventually evolved into.

At about the same time we launched our Q-Zoo, a national company called the American Comedy Network burst onto the scene. ACN supplied stations with a weekly shipment of pre-recorded humor ranging from parody songs to scripted character skits which you played back on the air and interacted with. At the time, this material was very fresh and very funny and it integrated seamlessly with the Zoo approach. Similarly, Rita Bentley and Mike Rivers also wrote scripts for their characters and Bob and I would interact live with them on the air. In the day-to-day presentation, there wasn't too much variation and I came to believe that finely honed scripts were *the* answer.

Pre-written punch lines were my world. But, then, many disc jockeys at that time subscribed to joke sheets - like mine. Beginning in Toledo at WOHO, I had been writing a monthly DJ joke sheet with the midday jock, Mike Morin, called "Dial-log" which we sold to hundreds of deejays across the country including (oh let me name drop) Howard Stern. He first subscribed in 1982 while he was at WWDC-FM in Washington, D.C. and continued to use our service for a while after he went to WNBC-AM, New York. But, Stern's act was also in transition and he was rapidly growing from a "jock" into a "shock jock" with little need for stupid one-liners.

As for me, I was still in punch line mode at Q94. Garet, on the other hand, was more spontaneous. Where I would labor the night before writing and perfecting a script, he would roll in 45 minutes before airtime, read the paper and scribble out some loosely crafted, hand-written outline of a bit.

This drove me nuts.

Garet was funny, homespun and very casual. I was just the opposite: high-strung, intense, perfection seeking and rigid.

You would think this would have made for a perfectly matched team since opposites are supposed to attract. But, it didn't. Don't misunderstand: we worked together successfully for a year-and-a-half. And as is customary in Radio, if a station can't beat you it tries to hire you.

At this point, EZ-104 was no longer a threat and rock station, WRXL-FM (XL-102), was having a hard time keeping its own footing. Then, one day Garet and I were invited to join the Program Director from XL-102 for a private lunch. Never one to turn down a free meal - and terribly curious as to why an archenemy would be feeding us - we met at the appointed time at a local hotel.

We were ushered into a small, private banquet room where we dined. The Program Director then said, "This is a one-time offer. And, if you mention this to anyone, I will deny it ever happened."

With that, he dropped two contracts down in front of us of offering each a starting salary of $50,000-a-year. He then added, "In addition, I'll provide you with a limo to work each day and before you start with us I'll fly you for a week to the island of your choice."

All he wanted from us was a commitment right there and then. If we walked out of the banquet room without signing, there was no deal.

Garet and I were quite complimented but a bit stunned. I was making a little over $30,000-a-year and I assume Garet had a similar deal. Fifty grand would have been a big leap for both of us, not to mention the other benefits. It would have been an easy transition since neither of us was under contract.

The Program Director left the room for a few minutes to let us discuss it. Although tempting, we ultimately decided against it because at that time, Q94 and the Q-Zoo were so well listened to and so prestigious, we didn't see how even the money and amenities could replace that.

It was sometime after that luncheon, being at the pinnacle of our success, I decided I was due a raise. I thought if I was so valuable to the competition, surely my own company would continue to appreciate my contribution to our achievements.

When Bob McNeil left Q94, Phil Goldman - a man who believed in promoting from within when possible - offered the Program Director's job to *"Bob-Alou"*. Bob-Alou was actually Bob Lewis. Well, that was his air name. His real name was Norman Freedlander. Bob-Alou had been with Q94, left to deejay in Chicago for a while and returned not long after I arrived.

Being my new immediate superior, he was the person who I had to go to for a raise. So, one day I walked in his office and gave him the pitch. I told him how I thought I had demonstrated my importance to the station. I thought I was worth a good raise. At that time, I was making $33,000-a-year, $3,000 more than when I had first arrived at Q94 a couple of years earlier.

Things didn't go the way I had hoped. Bob-Alou told me that I had pretty much reached the upper level of compensation. Sure, there might be a cost-of-living increase I could look forward to, but aside from that, I had pretty much hit the top rung.

With the gains I had made in Richmond and the professional acclaim our show had received, chances are I could have parlayed that success into years of stability there. Richmond was the kind of radio market where air-personalities could stay, even if they circulated from one station to another. Not all markets are like that. In some places, you're a one-time deal. Once you're fired or you quit a job, nobody else wants you; they're just happy you're out of the way.

Sometimes it's easier for Radio to just discard you. That would not have been the case in Richmond.

But, I was pretty pissed. I wanted recognition for my hard work and accomplishments. I wasn't thinking of the future, I was thinking about now. I had gone above and beyond. I had lived and slept the morning show. How could he so easily dismiss the countless all-night sessions I had spent in the production studio, creating elements for the Q-Zoo? There were plenty of nights when we had late appearances and instead of going home, I would go right to the station, shower there and go right to work again for the next morning's show. I was a tireless employee. I wanted some respect. And the way the business world shows you respect is by giving you money. That's the deal. That's why XL-102 made a run at us.

But in my own company, I felt patronized, disrespected, and taken for granted. In retrospect, I probably made one major error: followed the chain-of-command. Instead of accepting Bob-Alou's final word on the matter, what I should have done was gone over him straight to Goldman. But, I didn't. Later, when I eventually handed in my letter of resignation and explained my reasons, Phil simply said, "Why didn't you come to me?"

It was too late.

Soon after my meeting with Bob-Alou, I received a call from Alan Burns, a consultant. Burns contacted me on behalf of a "party" who was interested in talking to me about a job. It was all very secretive and covert; he wouldn't tell me any details, not even the name of the station. All that was missing was a disembodied voice saying, "Of course, Mr. Phelps, the tape of this conversation will self-destruct in 30 seconds. Good luck."

What did I have to lose? I agreed to meet with them. I received instructions to drive 90 minutes east to an expensive Norfolk restaurant where I met someone named Bob Canada. He was the Program Director of WNVZ-FM, a fledgling Top 40 station. The General Manager was Paul Todd.

By the end of dinner, they offered to double my salary. They wanted me to do whatever it was we had done in Richmond, only on their station.

How could I resist?

Chapter 11

In September of 1985, Bob Canada, my new boss, was quoted in the Hampton Roads *Daily Press* as saying, "Let's just say Corey's the highest paid DJ in the state of Virginia." I didn't know whether it was true or not but I liked the way it sounded. For better or for worse, I had begun to measure my success by income - not necessarily always the best standard to hold your life up to.

But, they doubled my salary to come to the Hampton Roads market and I went. Hampton Roads is a megalopolis: a very large urban complex involving several cities. It's comprised of Virginia Beach, Norfolk, Hampton, Suffolk and Chesapeake. My new station was physically located in and licensed to Virginia Beach but for ratings purposes was considered part of Norfolk, the 40th largest radio market. I signed a deal that started me off at $60,000-a-year with raises based on ratings performance. By the time I left, I was making around $74 grand. For that time, in that market, it was better than excellent compensation.

I moved to Virginia Beach and lived in a La Quinta Inn for the first 30 days. My wife, 8 1/2 months pregnant with our second child, Eric, stayed behind in Richmond to pack and get us ready for the transition. Besides, Chris wasn't about to up-and-move and have a baby in a strange city with doctors she didn't know. These were especially difficult days for her and the fact that she did not divorce me during this or any of our multitudes of moves is a testament to her strength. I was a good hour-and-a-half to her east and just prayed I would have enough time to get back for the birth when the time came.

The next couple of years were both triumphant and wrenching. I wasn't sure how to begin this part of my story until I received an email from a friend who sent me a link to an article in the online version of The *Virginian-Pilot*. It read in part:

Del Toro, radio 'shock jock,' found dead

Henry "The Bull" Del Toro, once a popular and controversial figure in Hampton Roads radio, was found dead Friday evening....of natural causes. In 1985, he pleaded guilty to cocaine charges. In 1993, he was convicted of prescription drug fraud...and ordered to undergo drug treatment and to perform community service....Del Toro left WNOR in 1995 to take on morning co-host duties at rival 96X WROX, but by then his ratings had peaked. He was fired two years later. Since then Del Toro's name surfaced from time to time, but the notoriety of his earlier years never returned.

Henry was 44 and this is his epitaph. He received a page-and-a-half as viewed through a web browser plus a small thumbnail photo.

I think the worst part about being successful is being forgotten.

I wonder if someday someone will write that I "surfaced from time to time".

Most radio personalities are just blips on a screen. We come, we go, and we drop under the radar. Stations change personnel all the time. Listeners hear us, listeners love us, and listeners forget us. We are interchangeable; an army of faceless voices providing the glue that holds radio formats together.

It takes an extraordinary air personality to inspire loyalty and build history with a listener. Once this bond is sealed, you would be hard-pressed to ever talk someone out of his or her listening preference or the homage each pays to their favorite deejay. Even so, time eventually erodes the shimmer and even the most notable DJs and hosts fade because listeners' lives go forward, while radio people remain behind, etched in a blurry, mental snapshot.

Part of the problem is we come free. Maybe that's why we're so easily discarded. A person can buy a wonderful book and cherish it their whole life. He may read it several times, loan it to a friend, or carefully store it on a shelf. But, hardly a soul records a radio program and does the same thing. There are coffee table books but no "coffee table radio shows". Nobody comes to your home, sits on your couch and picks up a broadcast.

Maybe that's partly why I'm writing this.

How terribly vain is it to hope that when it's all said and done, somebody will know you were here? For the last 25 years of my life, I have risen most days and been given the opportunity to shout out my presence as loud as my given wattage would allow me. This is a gift so few have. I should be grateful.

Yet, sometimes it is not enough. My voice is ephemeral. People are easily distracted and they forget. My worst fear is that I will not leave something worth remembering. It must be the most basic of instincts to want to leave a part of you behind as a marker. As humanity moves past where you once were, you hope it will at least acknowledge your existence for a moment, as it continues its perpetual push forward.

The first time I met Henry Del Toro was when I was making an appearance at a trade show just a couple of months after arriving at Z-104. I had been hammering him on the air, going for his jugular. He walked up to me, poked me in the chest, and said,

"You'll be gone in a year."

"We'll see about that," I responded.

He turned and walked away. It was obvious we were bitter rivals. Some time after that, my wife and I were strolling through a cemetery when we came upon a tombstone that was simply engraved "Bull". How could I resist? I took a photo of it and mailed it to Del Toro anonymously just to screw with his head. Given today's climate, that would probably be considered "terroristic threatening". At the very least, that kind of stunt would probably always land someone down at police headquarters under severe questioning.

In Richmond we had no qualms about attacking our competitor. You find his weakness and you start to re-position him. You change listeners' perceptions of him. It's a wonderful tactic we used successfully but it's a tricky one and can sometimes backfire.

You only attack your competitor when he is ahead of you in the ratings. You attack, hoping he'll respond. You appeal to his vanity and ego. You want him to tell his audience what little cockroaches you really are. You want him to come back at you with everything in his power because each time he mentions your name on his air, you win. When your competitor responds verbally, his listeners become curious and often switch over to hear just who this bastard is attacking their favorite deejay. Of course, that's when your door opens and it's up to you to go out there and convince them otherwise.

The first piece of the puzzle at the Z-Zoo was to go after Del Toro. His popularity and ratings were huge. To his credit, he *was* morning radio in Hampton Roads when I first arrived. The general comment I heard over and over again was simply that "nobody could knock him out of first place". It was unthinkable that anyone could successfully challenge him. Luckily, I was just cocky enough not to believe this.

Since Henry was considered "untouchable", the fact that I was gunning for him got around. As soon as Del Toro acknowledged me, the battle became fierce. Over time, the strategy worked well enough to raise my profile and punch holes in his. That was the first step to success.

But, even with all the acrid on-air exchanges, it was never personal between Henry and me, at least not from my point of view. I was simply the executioner sent to chop off another head. The executioner is not emotionally involved. He is just following orders.

My first on-air partner was Dave Sanborn, a nice guy who had been doing another shift on the station. Bob Canada, who was fired/resigned (take your pick) a couple of months after I got there, had just enough time to hire Liz York who possessed a smooth and sensual news voice and Michael Creasy, a cheerful fellow who was asked to produce us. Mary Ann Rayment, an assistant to Canada, contributed some quirky voices for some characters I created.

The point was to replicate the Richmond Q-Zoo in Hampton Roads, or at least take the formula and create a Z-Zoo based closely on its success. I did this fastidiously. Of course, I was now copying a copy we made from the original Q-Zoo in Tampa. Stealing in Radio is about as prevalent as cavities in Appalachia. There is no shame in it. There is only shame in losing the ratings race.

I arranged for Rita Bentley to be hired to phone us with her *Susan B. Anthony Jones* character made so popular on Q94. I recreated the popular *Mr. Leonard* Q-Zoo character which Bob McNeil had lifted from the Tampa Zoo. Jingles, sound effects, music beds - everything I could think of was transferred or modified to fit the Z Morning Zoo at Z-104.

Rick Sklar, the station's consultant, met with me several times the first few months and we reviewed the new Zoo and plotted strategy. Sklar was the legendary programmer behind WABC-AM in New York when it was a monster Top 40 outlet. Ironically, this was the station I grew up with, listening to "Cousin' Brucie" late at night in my room as a child. Sklar began there in 1963 and helped propel WABC to the #1 Top 40 station the country with 6 million listeners-a-week. I was in awe of him and a bit intimidated. He was a brilliant and successful guy and it was an honor working with him.

I don't remember the exact date in September of 1985 when we unveiled the new Z Morning Zoo, but I do remember September 24. The show had been on the air maybe three weeks. Hurricane Gloria was heading up the Atlantic coast and at its peak. Now, a category 4 storm, it was several hundred miles off the east coast of Florida with sustained winds of 143 miles-per-hour. The weather models indicated there was a possibility it would hit us.

A few minutes before 6 a.m. that morning, my wife called me at the station.

"My water broke," she said. "I'm going to the hospital. Come home."

I jumped into my car and raced back to Richmond. My second child, Eric, was about to arrive and I needed to be there. It would take a good hour-and-a-half to two hours, depending on the traffic. I barely made it. Chris gave birth within 30 minutes of my arrival.

I stayed in Richmond two days before returning to Virginia Beach. Luckily, my parents - who had moved to Richmond after my first son, David, was born - were there to help her. It should have been me, but I felt an obligation to be back at the station in the event "Gloria" hit Hampton Roads. This was an unfair choice for me to have to make and even more unfair for my wife to have to endure.

By September 27, the storm had passed near Cape Henry as a category 3 hurricane, gusting up to 104 miles-per-hour. It caused $5.5 million dollars damage in Virginia and left 300,000 people without power in Hampton Roads. The staff at Z-104 did what was necessary to keep the information flowing.

Building a new morning show can be a daunting task. I had never done it by myself and the pressure was enormous. But, that's why these people had hired me and doubled my salary. I remember sitting in my motel room the first few weeks wondering if I had made the right decision. It wasn't so much the task ahead as it was the security I had left behind. I was riddled with doubts.

Anytime you leave people you know for those you don't, it's natural to suffer from some xenophobia. But, by now, I had also taken enough new jobs to realize that the majority of my darkest thoughts generally occurred late at night, alone in a motel room, and in a strange city.

My solution was to sleep during the day and work all night. I would go to bed at 11 a.m. and sleep until around six in the evening. After dinner or breakfast - I'm not sure which one to call it - I would begin reading newspapers, watching TV and preparing for the next day's show.

About 1 or 2 a.m. I would head into the station and spend several hours producing bits for the show. I kept this schedule until Chris arrived and we moved into our new apartment.

When the first rating period, fall 1986, ended, I was sure the new Z Morning Zoo would demonstrate commendable progress. Imagine my shock when the book came back and our ratings dropped! I was aghast. A pit opened wide in my stomach. I could not believe it and went into a depression. What I did not recognize, initially, was how different from Q94 this situation was.

When I came to Richmond, I was smoothly integrated into an already fairly successful morning show on an established station. But, Z-104 was a poorly constructed Top 40 station struggling at about 10th place in the market. The people who were listening in the morning were only there for the music and listeners are usually not good with change.

Our new show's chatter and comedy pretty much annoyed whatever audience had been there. Very few people - "frequency sitters" as I call them - will blindly stay tuned to a radio station after a major programming change. New morning shows often wind up cleansing the time slot. I had been through this before and at the time, only understood the outcome in terms of a failure. To his credit, the General Manager, Paul Todd, anticipated this and convinced me I was on the right track.

The first cast of the Z Morning Zoo didn't last very long. Things began to change when Bob Canada left the station. To this day, I really don't know the circumstances of his departure. What I do know is Canada, in my opinion, was a strange guy. He wore expensive suits and flashy clothing, drove a big, oversized luxury car, lived in what I thought was a gaudily decorated apartment and talked more like a bookie than a Program Director. Actually, he reminded me of a small time mobster, like the character "Carbone" from the movie *Goodfellas*.

One day he was Program Director and the next day he was gone.

Paul Todd didn't want to say much at all. Mary Ann Rayment, who worked closely with Canada, was tight-lipped, too. I never again saw his name in a trade newspaper, heard it muttered, or ran into anyone who knew his whereabouts. Maybe he rotated one-too many songs too quickly and now slept with the fishies. The disappearance of labor leader Jimmy Hoffa and Bob Canada: two of the 20th century's most notorious mysteries.

Z-104 was in transition and apparently, I was the first shot fired over the bow. One of the personalities working there when I arrived was a deejay named "Shane Brother Shane". He was older than I was and was holding down the early evening shift. We became somewhat friendly for a time and what struck me most about Shane was how similar he was to Dan, that lonely, lost guy who I worked with at WTGC-AM in Lewisburg, Pennsylvania.

Shane had been one of the top radio personalities in the state of New York during the 1960s and 1970s at stations like WGR, WKBW, and WWKB. But, now he was struggling to put his life back together. His wife and he had split and Shane was starting over in a strange city. I remember sitting in his living room one night, listening to him spill his guts about how he and his old lady just couldn't keep it together anymore. I don't know if it was his fault, her fault or both their faults. Most likely it was Radio's fault.

All that was left now was this modest apartment and the gig at Z-104 which he took in an attempt to try to rehabilitate his career. There was no doubt he was a short-timer. He just wanted to score high enough ratings to somehow get back on the air in Buffalo, where he was known and loved. I felt badly for him. Here was this older guy with a worn and weathered face, playing records for 12-year-olds in a town where he didn't mean shit.

I didn't want that to be me. Ever.

Radio has so many lonely people who drift in-and-out of cities and in between jobs. All of us have our personal reasons for being on the air. Some seek approval, some seek love, some are compelled to nurture egos that could not survive in the everyday work world, and some of us just hide. They're the saddest of all. They use Radio to shield themselves from divorces, deaths, diseases, denials, losses, and failures.

Shane Brother Shane left Hampton Roads within a year from when I first met him.

Like Bob Canada, I don't know where he went next or whatever happened to him. The most recent online reference I could find, from 1999, said he was participating in a "Rock and Roll Radio Reunion" on WHTT-FM, an oldies station in Buffalo, New York. I hope he got back to where he needed to be - or at least was able to find comfort in staying where he might have had to settle on being. Shane used to end his programs by saying, "Make the peace, share the peace, keep the peace..."

Maybe he found his.

After some searching a new Program Director was hired. It was one of those situations where it had already been ordained that Dave Sanborn probably was not going to work out and whoever the new P.D. was, he would be joining me as co-host - "...but only with my blessing, of course". That's the kind of thing management types say to air talent when they know damn well it's *not* going to matter what you really think.

So, I had a new partner.

I've thought about this guy on-and-off over the years and now that I have the opportunity to put it all into words, I'm stumped as to where to begin. Let me start this way: when a woman tells you she has a bad feeling about someone, listen to her.

I didn't.

From the very first time my wife met this guy, she did not like him. Call it a woman's intuition. She told me. She warned me. I wasn't convinced. Or maybe I just wanted to try to make the best of a situation. After all, I had just signed a contract, sold my home, left many friends, and moved 90 miles to take a job where the Program Director vanished within 60 days of my arrival and the personnel on my morning show completely rolled over within the first 4 months. Not to mention my career had been threatened by Del Toro as having one year to live. This business is about change and few choices. My only other option would have been to tuck myself into a corner and curl up in a fetal position.

So, I adapted. The first indication I was in for problems was when my new on-air partner said he wanted to run the "board". A board is another name for the console which mixes the sound from microphones and other sound sources like recorded audio, CDs, etc. This is important so, let me take a moment to explain.

Every morning show needs an anchor and he usually runs the board. The anchor decides direction or at least makes decisions - some technical - that keep the show moving ahead. The anchor guides the other players toward resolution in bits, conversation and the like. The anchor knows when to "dump" out from whatever the show is doing at any given moment and move on. The anchor makes sure the commercials are played; the news gets on, the traffic reports air on time, etc. After a song, the anchor establishes the break, says the station name, does the time and basically acts as the aural structure or framework of the show. In a Zoo-type show, the anchor also was responsible for inserting the goofy sound effects, music beds, etc.

The anchor is the audio architect for the program and only one person can be the anchor. That doesn't necessarily mean the other guy is relegated to just being a sidekick. On the contrary: you can still have two co-hosts. You just can't paddle in different directions.

Every ship has one captain, every police department has one chief, and every radio show should have one anchor.

If two people are trying to be the anchor, there will be conflict, such as two decisions being made at the same time or two sound elements being played simultaneously. Who decides when something ends? When something starts? Which way to go?

My partner did not want to defer to me at first. But, I was hired to anchor the show and I was not willing to place the fate of this new program and my reputation for running it in the hands of someone I just met. Unfortunately, I did not win this battle.

My new partner argued he should have a "mini console" at his disposal that plugged into the main console. From there, he also could run music beds, sound effects, and sound bites whenever he felt it appropriate. He was the Program Director and he got his way. In my opinion, it was sheer unmitigated ego.

So, that's the foot we started off on - and eventually that foot would be stuck in his mouth so deep we would both suffer the consequences.

Oddly, though, as different as we were (I was normal and he was possessed by Satan), we managed to work well enough together to create #1 ratings. It was sheer luck that our personalities meshed into one cohesive unit that worked together on a daily basis.

I won't say my new partner wasn't talented because he was. What he brought to our mix was similar to what Bob McNeil brought to the Richmond Zoo. He was the one who stepped further out, said ruder things, made really crass comments and in general created trouble. I, again, was the balance, a very comfortable role for me. We did some great things together: originated a "Kidwatch" program throughout the Hampton Roads area to protect children, supported multiple charitable

Corey Deitz

events, lent cheer and support to Navy families with sailors out to sea and much more.

On May 25, 1986, over 5,600,000 people donated 10 bucks apiece and held hands over a 4,124-mile route in a national event called "Hands Across America". The money went toward the homeless problem. Our show had the power to pull 8,000 listeners to the Virginia Beach oceanfront to participate in the local version. Certainly, the Z-104 Zoo would not have been as successful without my partner.

We also would not have been sued for $1,000,000 if it weren't for him. At least that's the way I see it.

The day that we were served with the lawsuit is etched quite clearly in my mind. It was a little after 9 a.m. and the radio station had just changed ownership. The new company, S&F Communications had literally just taken over *that* very day. Paul Todd was out as General Manager and a new guy was in. Talk about timing for a lawsuit to be served.

Suddenly, a sheriff's deputy walked into the control room and handed me some papers. At first, I wasn't sure what it was. I thought it was a joke. Then my jaw dropped. When we got off the air, the very first interaction with our new General Manager was to inform him that we were being sued. It was not just the company, either. Both my partner and I were personally named in the lawsuit. I was pretty freaked out. I didn't know a thing about the law. I just knew I did not have $1,000,000 dollars. The Associated Press reported it this way in November, 1986:

On-air comments by radio station announcers about a death sentence for two dogs in September is the basis for a judge's $1 million libel suit against the announcers and their radio station.

In papers filed in Virginia Beach Circuit Court yesterday, General District Substitute Judge W. Brantley Basnight III alleged that two announcers at WNVZ-FM and the owners of the station maliciously attacked him on the radio after he ordered the dogs destroyed Sept. 2.

The suit contends that during their early morning radio show, the [DJs]...repeatedly called Basnight "stupid", "redneck" and "Judge Assnight."

"The statements were false, defamatory and insulting...malicious, slanderous, libelous and...tended to violence and breach of the peace," according to the papers.

Boy, is that a mouthful of legal bullshit or what? Of course, anyone can sue anyone else for practically anything. If the suit isn't thrown out by a judge for being frivolous and winds up going forward, the person suing has to prove the charges and damages resulting from the actions.

My on-air partner should have known where the line was, but he apparently didn't. It was he who referred to the judge as "Assnight" and a "redneck". I corrected him, tongue-in-cheek, on the "Assnight" pronunciation. That was my job. I was the balance. I'm sure I agreed the decision itself was "stupid" but that was about the extent of my guilt.

Most would argue that this was typical morning radio patter and given the context of our show and the fact that the judge was a public figure, our indiscretions weren't that egregious. We really had the first Amendment on our side because in the end, ninety percent of it was just opinion. It was that additional gray ten percent which was troubling and open to interpretation. It didn't matter. We had a judge on our asses, with a lawsuit in his circuit and the plaintiff was among friends.

The lawsuit hung over my wife and me until I left Z-104. There was a point where Chris and I actually discussed getting a divorce and putting all our money and belongings in her name just so that if it came to a judgment against me, we wouldn't lose everything we had.

There were interviews, depositions, discovery and many letters from lawyers. I kept all the papers and have it nicely tucked away as a reminder that at one time, somebody actually thought I was worth a million dollars. It never went to trial. The lawyers faxed each other documents for a couple of years and got plenty of billable hours out of it. In the end, I was informed the judge settled for a few thousand dollars. I think the lawyers did better than he did.

It was probably the lawsuit that pushed me over the edge with my partner. I was angry and blamed him for finally going too far. Our relationship had slowly started to unravel and after a couple of years together, I was becoming progressively unhappy with my association with him.

My situation at Z-104 evolved into just the opposite of Richmond. In Richmond, I wasn't making the money I felt I deserved but I was getting the recognition. In Virginia Beach, I was making the money I wanted but was not getting the recognition I deserved. The fact of the matter is my partner began to take credit for things he should not have. More specifically, my ideas. Not only was that wrong, but his ego was pissing off my ego.

There seems to be two kinds of people in this business: the group who fall victim to some bizarre *Radio Bermuda Triangle* and suddenly vanish, like Bob Canada, never to be heard from again and a second collection of wanderers who you just can't seem to shake, no matter how many cities you move to. And despite how often this second group fucks up radio stations, how many people they alienate, step on, mentally abuse, use as scapegoats, and lie to, they keep being hired - and usually into management positions - as Program Directors. They cling to this business like dog shit on a shoe.

My wife once said "All radio stations are toilets – they just flush differently."

This is usually the reason.

I started to look for a new job. Again.

Chapter 12

I had begun sending airchecks and resumes to opportunities that looked promising. At the time (pre-Internet for the masses, when spam was something you still ate on Boy Scout hikes), most employment opportunities appeared in a trade newspaper called *Radio & Records*. When someone placed a want ad in *R&R* and they didn't want you to know who they were, the ad was often posted with a "blind" box number.

The radio business is somewhat sneaky this way. There's this "executioner" mentality that pervades management. It probably stems from the fact that in no other business, except maybe television, does an employee have access to so many people with the ability to do so much damage. Management wants to prevent the guy who they plan on firing from getting wind of it because the last thing higher-ups want to hear on the radio station is the afternoon deejay saying something like, "These fuckers are gonna' fire my ass. Can you believe it? What a bunch of ungrateful pricks". Yeah, that can cause a few public relations problems.

In a way I understand this thinking because I've definitely met my share of mental cases who masquerade as radio personalities. I, too, have been suddenly yanked off the air and replaced several times but it still pisses me off because I don't like being treated like a nominee for a strait jacket. But, most managers assume every on-air performer should be handled as if he was two days off his Ritalin.

So, blind box ads have commonly be used to keep things covert. Naturally, not knowing whom the materials were really going to could backfire in several ways:

1. You might be applying for a position at your own station which would immediately anger your Program Director upon his finding out you were looking to leave.
2. You might be sending your materials to somebody who was a friend of your Program Director and also aware you worked for him. Again, you'd be busted.
3. Worse yet: your materials could wind up going to your competition and they would assuredly start the rumor that you were unhappy and looking to leave which would surely find you, once again,

sitting in your Program Director's office having to explain it all.

Chances of sitting in the Program Director's office during any job search were always about twenty percent by my estimate.

But, these were just the chances you had to take under the system in place. One blind box ad I sent my materials to happen to wind up on the desk of consultant Walter Sabo. He evidently liked something he heard because he called and wanted to know if I would be interested in working in Chicago, the country's 3rd largest radio market.

My jaw dropped.

"Of course," I said.

This sounded too good to actually happen. I was convinced if I really accepted that it *might*, I would no doubt jinx it into oblivion. Often, when we want something badly, our inner voice begins a dialogue with our emotions, preparing them for the possibility of inevitable disappointment. It's a defense mechanism we all employ. It plays to the side of us that expects defeat. We are conditioned early on to accept that life is not fair and "you can't always get what you want". So, I sublimated my excitement down to a level of daily control and the process began, all along thinking it would never come to fruition.

The first thing the needed from me was more tapes. Raw tapes. Unedited tapes. To a Radio personality, sending raw tapes is like running through the *Radio Job Gauntlet of Doom*. Raw tapes mean the consultant or Program Director is going to hear every single solitary screw-up, mistake, idiosyncratic or dumb ass comment you make.

They ask for raw tapes because they want to hear how you sound "un-doctored". The Program Director wants to hear consistency and also wants to confirm that the aircheck you sent was indicative of your daily performance, not some glorious moment of genius you happen to record.

With raw audio it's a certainty whoever is listening is going to hear each technical error. Like when you turn your microphone off before you spit out the last syllable. Or when you press buttons that don't start things. Like when you take live phone calls from people who are actually trying to dial, say, your competition for some contest and instead call you by mistake.

The Program Director wants to know how you deal with these snafus while on the air. "SNAFU" is an acronym which was often used by soldiers in World War II. It stands for: **S**ituation **N**ormal **A**ll **F**ucked **U**p. Having worked in dozens of radio studios, I can assure you that there are always snafus. Equipment breaks down, buttons don't work, computers lock up, the copy is wrong, the recorded promo that's running on the air is outdated, the telephone interface is on the blink and you can't get calls on the air, etc. If you make a mistake or a technical issue interferes with your performance, the Program Director wants to know how you deal with it and then move on because it's guaranteed you *will* have snafus at his station or any other. SNAFU could also easily stand for: **S**tation **N**ormal **A**ll **F**ucked **U**p.

The raw audio shows whether you're the real deal or not. Airchecks get their attention but, if you can't deliver you will not last.

Never send an aircheck you can't live up to. True, an aircheck must be exemplary but never send one that your live performance couldn't rival on a good day. A Program Director will accept an off day, once-in-a-while, but will quickly notice inconsistent performance.

When magnetic tape was still used to send airchecks, as opposed to CDs or .mp3 files, a peculiar phenomenon occurred sometimes and it once happened to me. The mechanical performance of reel-to-reel tape recorders and cassette decks could easily vary from machine to machine. Sometimes, this would show itself in the playback of a tape on the receiver's end.

For instance, when I arrived to begin my job in Toledo the Program Director immediately commented on how my voice sounded deeper on the tape. After some thought I realized his cassette deck must have been running slower than the one I used to make copies of my aircheck, making my voice sound ballsier. For some time afterwards, I was a bit uncomfortable, thinking the Program Director felt I had somehow deceived him. In the end, my performance eliminated any doubt that I was right for the job. Today, digital technology has all but eliminated the possibility of such audio quirks unless someone consciously employs a pitch trick.

My tapes were sent FedEx to the Program Director of WFYR-FM, John Wetherbee, who after some consideration called and asked me to fly up. I spent a day with John, met the General Manager, Dick Rakovan, toured the city, made my pitch and heard his.

Then the wait.

Wetherbee was in the process of filling both morning and afternoon drive positions on WFYR, a property owned by RKO General. WFYR or *"FIRE"* as it was sometimes pronounced on the air (sometimes even referred to as *"The Great Chicago Fire"*), was an oldies station which was more or less limping along, with its glory days some years behind it.

Wetherbee's morning drive decision had come down to a choice between Larry Dixon, a successful Dallas personality and me. After what I'm sure was at least a week of silence from Chicago, the phone rang and Wetherbee offered me the afternoon slot. He told me it would start at $90,000 dollars-a-year. I was momentarily disappointed it was not mornings but that quickly passed. To be honest, I would have spit-shined shoes in the sales department just to work at a Chicago radio station.

"Absolutely," I said.

But, it wasn't quite an offer - yet. There was a small, legal glitch. The lawyers for WFYR said Wetherbee technically could not present a written offer to me or sign anything between us until I was out from under my contract with Z-104. As a matter of fact, the discussions we had up to this point didn't really exist (wink wink). They didn't want to be sued and it was a valid concern. Stations steal talent from other stations all the time. It usually only matters if the talent being stolen has great ratings and matters even more when the theft is perpetrated within the same city. I was assured this was only a formality and as soon as I obtained a release from my current contract, we could do the deal.

In the meantime, I hired a lawyer, Wayne Souza, who began quiet negotiations on my behalf. The guy was worth every penny. Not only was he broadcast savvy, but he worked hard to protect me. The real value of his services will become apparent a little later.

Over the years, I have pondered how the next set of events unfolded. In retrospect, I'm sure I handled them badly. By the time the Chicago opportunity came along, I was disgusted with my partner in Virginia Beach and wasn't a big fan of the General Manager, either. Both men had inherited me and vice versa. When Paul Todd, the former G.M of Z-104 signed my contract, he was happy to pay me an excellent salary for results achieved.

On the other hand, the man who succeeded him made no secret of the fact that he didn't like my deal. There was tension, even though the morning ratings were outstanding. By the way, I think this goes back to the point I made earlier about how some people in management don't quite understand why talent is paid - and sometimes very well - for what it is we do. I think it's especially prevalent in situations where the morning deejay makes more money than the General Manager, which I believe was at the heart of my situation at Z-104.

My dilemma was this: Was there enough friction between the two of us that the General Manager would see my desire to leave as a gift or would he put aside his personal feelings and deny me a release so as not to disrupt the morning show.

Then, an incident which occurred on the air lent itself to my ultimate disassociation with Z-104. On October 22, 1988, we were doing our show as usual when a call came in from a listener. Here's how one local newspaper reported it:

A woman claimed some black students at Bayside Junior High School had declared Friday "Kill Whitey Day." She said her brother, a police officer, had warned her to keep her children home because racial tensions were high."

...Soon another caller, this time a young girl, told the same story. [Other Deejay] said the idea was "disgusting." "I certainly hope this is not true," Deitz said.

By 9 a.m., the station had broadcast about 40 calls from parents and students. Suddenly the radio station was in the middle of a controversy. The calls, totaling about 200, continued after the program ended.

I have news clippings from *"The Virginian Pilot"*, *"The Ledger Star"* and *"The Daily Press"*, all of which reported the incident. Unfortunately, because of bad scrapbook keeping, I cannot attribute the above quote to a specific paper so I have listed them all. Whichever it was, please accept the acknowledgement.

There was a general outcry, mostly from parents and school administrators. They accused my partner, Z-104, and me as having acted irresponsibly in airing the calls. We were blamed for "fanning the flames" of racial tension. People threatened to bring in the F.C.C. which they did (who later absolved us of any wrongdoing). Ultimately, the school principal sent home a note to parents assuring them the school was not dangerous. Newspaper headlines abounded:

"Rumors of racial conflict mar school day"

"Junior high school becomes hot topic for radio callers"

"Fear, allegations of violence erupt at Bayside Junior High PTA meeting"

It was quite a media circus. In retrospect, the content we aired that morning was typical radio fodder by today's standards. Yes, it was controversial, but it was also compelling. Whether it was really "Kill Whitey Day" is irrelevant. It was an important topic to our listeners and they wanted to talk about the rumors they had heard. They wanted to express their fears and concerns. Either way - to them - it was real. This was great radio.

Certainly, it was blown out of proportion and a lot of pressure was brought to bear on the station. So much, in fact, that the General Manager called an afternoon meeting for the morning show to talk more about it.

This, I thought to myself, was the opportunity I was looking for.

What I am about to tell you, I have never told anyone except for my wife and my lawyer at the time, Wayne Souza.

I knew the meeting was going to be emotional and tense and decided I might be able to use it to my advantage. I figured if I pushed the G.M.'s buttons just right, he would get so pissed off, he would fire me and I would get my release.

I was right.

We began talking about what had occurred earlier in the day. My stance was that we had done nothing wrong. The General Manager, who did not trust us, began insisting that from now on, we call him - at home - before airing controversial calls.

"You have got to be kidding me," I said.

He wasn't. I really *was* getting pissed.

Just as an aside, anyone who has done a morning show or other high-profile radio program that utilizes callers must quickly recognize how stupid an idea this really was. First of all, that's why radio shows have phone screeners. They are the first defense in weeding out crackpots and weirdoes, which oddly enough, most shows today encourage to call.

You do not tie the hands of a radio personality in the way the Z-104 General Manager was suggesting. It's utterly ridiculous to try and micro-manage a radio show like that. How do you know in *advance* a call is going to become controversial? Who the fuck did he think was running the morning show? The gang from Miss Cleo's Psychic Hotline?

His demand was so ludicrous, so moronic, so completely out-of-touch with the dynamics of a radio show, I doubt you would find one General Manager or Program Director in Radio today who would agree with it.

If I hadn't gone into that meeting wanting to piss him off, I certainly didn't need any incentive now.

We began to argue. Emotions flared. The General Manager was yelling at me and I was yelling back. Finally, it peaked in a crescendo of insult when I just blurted out, "FUCK YOU."

Oh fuck. The fuck word. Now I was really fucked!

"Fuckin' A," I thought to myself. Fuck-head took the bait.

I quietly waited for his reaction.

Then the significance of the moment took hold. It was as if Kyle and Eric from *South Park* had just yelled, "You bastard! You killed Kenny!"

The General Manager was visibly red and it looked as if his head was about to explode. You would have sworn the Discovery Channel was there filming the first actual human volcano. I think lava was, in fact, coming out of his mouth. In an eruption to rival Mt. St. Helens, pieces of flaming words spewed out from in between his lips as he threw me out of the building.

Like I said, he wasn't crazy about my deal and probably patted himself on the back for quite a while afterwards for finally unloading my financial overhead. Later that day, he called me and told me to be in his office the next day. Obviously, he fired me. He never knew I set him up.

I was thrilled. Oddly though, when I think back, I sometimes wonder under what clause in my contract he found as a reason to actually fire me. I'm not sure "fuck you" was legally enough to do the trick. My lawyer even suggested we might sue for breach of contract but I didn't care at this point. All I wanted now was my written release.

The next day I received it but the General Manager was still emitting volcanic ash and smoke from his ears so instead of sticking to the subject, he used the opportunity to paint a very negative portrait of me within the document based solely on the "fuck you" theory of character assassination.

Today, an employer wouldn't do that for legal reasons - the fear of being sued - but he wanted anyone who read this release to know just what a scumbag he thought I was. You must understand, "fuck you" is akin to a *Gauntlet of Defiance* being thrown down. Defying management is always interpreted as the ultimate outrage to its ego. At this point, it wasn't business for him, it was personal.

Initially, I didn't think the wording mattered much assuming the Chicago folks would be more interested in the big picture. Besides, they had already met with me and knew I wasn't some lunatic. So, I immediately faxed my release to John Wetherbee in Chicago, thinking I was home free. What I should have done was explain at that very moment just how my release came about. It probably would have short-circuited the problems about to occur.

A couple of hours later, John called and said, "There's a problem." Apparently, the lawyers for RKO, the parent company of WFYR, were very concerned about the wording in my release. Not knowing me personally or being privy to the situation under which I won my release, the document made me out to be less than acceptable employee.

I explained to Wetherbee what had taken place. I told him it was all a "show" to obtain the release. He was cool about it but said he would have to discuss it with the lawyers and with Dick Rakovan, the General Manager. John said it might be the next day until he got back to me.

Well, this was a very sobering moment. I had just gotten myself fired from what had evolved into a $74,000-a-year paycheck and my next gig was, all-of-a-sudden, quite up in the air.

Quite frankly, I was never so scared in all my life. I had an expensive mortgage on a house in a private golf club community, two young children, no other income and no money to speak of in savings. What was I thinking? Why did I go and do that? My wife and I spent the whole night awake and second-guessing my actions in between bouts of prayers and tears. The only liquor in the house was a bottle of vodka. I drank it.

In my darkest moment, a voice I did not expect called. It was Henry "The Bull" Del Toro. He called to lend his support and to blast my company for the dismissal. I was almost shocked to hear from him, remembering how he had confronted me two years earlier and forewarned my demise. Maybe he was happy to just be getting rid of me, or it might have just been that Henry was a decent guy after all. I wasn't sure.

But, quite surprisingly, even after I left for my new job in Chicago, Del Toro continued to phone my wife to make sure she was okay and to see if she needed anything. Henry really did care. How ironic. When you least expect it, the one you thought was your enemy, turns into a friend you never considered. How wonderful to know life provides such surprises. I cannot offer any explanation as to how the wheel turned in a way that would have brought out this type of outreach. I can only attribute it to the type of respect warriors hold for each other after realizing each is a worthy opponent.

Waiting for the final word from Chicago was emotionally brutal. At the same time I was receiving much support from friends along with many calls from newspapers and TV stations. The phone rang endlessly. I was too consumed with anxiety to give statements to the media. I asked my lawyer, Wayne, to speak on my behalf.

Helpful Hint: If you are ever fired amidst controversial conditions, *do not* ask your lawyer to speak for you as it is terribly expensive every time he opens his mouth. If he offers "spokesperson" services - and you think you must have them - ask if the "no comment" option is available.

This is the most affordable because, as you know, attorneys charge for every minute of their time. Every second of every minute. This means the less they say, the more you can afford to have them continue to say nothing on your behalf. And remember: if they fax out a statement that says you have "no comment", they will charge you for the call, the fax paper, the electricity to run the fax machine, the depreciation of the fax machine, and the time it took to dictate to someone that you have "no comment". So, make sure they say "no comment" in person to whoever needs an official "no comment" for their newspaper or television news story.

Basically, it is very expensive to *not* say anything through a lawyer. You are better off using the money to buy a good bottle of Cuervo, drinking half of it, and then just saying any damn thing you want to the media.

The next day, Wetherbee called to tell me the lawyers understood the situation, didn't think I was an axe murderer or anarchist, and it was okay to finish the deal with me. I was ecstatic, mostly because I wasn't going to be homeless.

To celebrate, Chris and I rented a limo and invited five neighbors we were most friendly with to have dinner on us. After all, my yearly salary was about to jump to $90,000. I could afford it.

Ironically, a couple of days after surviving the near loss of the WFYR job, I received a call from WCKG-FM, another Chicago station. They were interested in me for their morning show but I was already mentally committed to WFYR, and somewhat grateful for having that gig. My sense of loyalty is strong and even though I wasn't yet under contract, I kind of blew them off. In retrospect, I should have pursued it further.

Never limit your possibilities.

We had some language to iron out and my lawyer played phone tag with the RKO lawyers for days, trying to get the deal done. WFYR was hoping to have me start within a week to ten days. Finally, I told Wetherbee I was just going to pack up and drive to Chicago and assume the paperwork would be worked out by the time I was supposed to go on the air.

He agreed to this. Two days later, I kissed Chris goodbye and set out for Illinois with all my belongings tied down in the bed of a pickup truck with no cap on the bed.

I must have looked like I had been separated from Uncle Jed, Granny, Jethro, and Ellie Mae.

At the end of my first day on the road, I stopped at a motel to get some sleep. Since everything I owned was tied down in the back of my truck, I had to move everything inside my room for the night. The next morning, I got up, reloaded and repacked the truck, and finished the trip to Chicago.

Chicago is a big city and if you've never been there before, it's easy to get lost. My first mistake was exiting off I-90 too early. As I left the exit ramp and entered this run down neighborhood, an old song by Jim Croce, *Bad Bad Leroy Brown* began to play on my radio:

"The South Side of Chicago is the meanest part of town

And if you go down there, you better just beware

Of a man called Leroy Brown"

No sooner had I heard these lyrics, than I suddenly realized I *was* on the South Side of Chicago, at a stop light, surrounded by four street corners full of gang members, sitting in a pickup truck with my stuff hanging out the back. This could not good.

"I'm going to die," I thought to myself.

"They're going to kill me right here, fence my belongings, burn my truck, drag my broken redneck ass up Michigan Avenue and deposit me at the front door of Marshall Fields with a sign around my neck that says "Did you lose a honky?"

As soon as the light turned, I raced up the road and did not look back.

Welcome to Chicago.

Chapter 13

WFYR-FM in Chicago was owned by RKO General. The company's beginnings dated to 1882 with ownership of one humble vaudeville theater. As more theaters were added, the chain grew and became the Keith-Albee-Orpheum theaters. Then, in 1928, David Sarnoff, the Chairman of RCA (Radio Corporation of America), got together with Joseph P. Kennedy, John F. Kennedy's father, to promote a business deal which combined the Keith-Albee-Orpheum theater chain with Pathe Studios and Kennedy's own Film Booking Office of America. This accountant's nightmare became the Radio-Keith-Orpheum Corporation - or RKO.

Considering David Sarnoff's power at the time, it's easy to understand why "Radio" got first billing. Unfortunately, nobody seems to know what happened to "Albee". I suspect if you find Bob Canada - you will also find him.

The new RKO Corporation branched out and starting making movies to show in its huge string of theaters. RKO began calling its cinematic creations "Radio Pictures" in the hopes of garnering positive marketing appeal by positioning itself next to the hottest communication technology of the time. The company was very successful in the movie business and is most notably remembered for the Orson Welles classic, *Citizen Kane,* Frank Capra's *It's A Wonderful Life, The Hunchback of Notre Dame,* and many more remarkable films.

The eccentric billionaire, Howard Hughes, purchased RKO in 1948. He proceeded to screw it up for several years until he sold it for $25 million dollars in the early 1950s. The buyer was General Tire and Rubber Company and between its new acquisition and the broadcast holdings it already had, everything melted into a media pot that was finally distilled down to RKO General.

One other notable fact from history: what is affectionately known as *"Boss Radio"* began in 1965 on an RKO station in Los Angeles, KHJ-AM. The "Boss Radio" concept dominated Top-40 Radio in the 1960s and 1970s. Even today, some Oldies formatted Radio stations still emulate this classic presentation.

Indeed, RKO General had a rich heritage, especially in Radio. By the time I got to WFYR-FM, little did I know what a screwed-up mess the parent company and their broadcast properties were in. You would have thought Howard Hughes was running it again.

It seems as far back as 1965, RKO General was facing numerous investigations over its business and financial practices. Then, in 1969, the company applied for license renewal for its Boston television property, WNAC-TV. For some reason, the F.C.C decided to base the renewals of *all* of RKO's other stations on the outcome of the WNAC proceeding.

Through numerous hearings and appeals, the issue lingered into the 1970s and was ultimately decided in 1981. December 4 of that year, the Appeals Court ruled against RKO on WNAC-TV's license renewal. Things got worse. While all this was going on with the F.C.C, the Securities and Exchange Commission had also been entertaining complaints and was considering allegations against RKO for securities fraud.

General Tire, a subsidiary of RKO, admitted to financial irregularities. It seems the company was trying to hide illegal political contributions and bribes it had paid to foreign officials. The situation became even more volatile because RKO General had been denying these same allegations to the F.C.C. Naturally, the F.C.C. got pretty pissed off and subsequently ruled RKO unfit to be a broadcast licensee, stripping it of all its TV licenses. In addition, RKO was ordered to dispose of all its other broadcast properties.

RKO's lawyers managed to tie up the divestiture process for eight more years with legal and procedural actions until 1990, when its final station, KHJ-TV, was sold, thus ending the RKO broadcast media empire.

I assure you; I was not given this history lesson during my job interview.

Radio is an oddly convoluted entity which doesn't always operate by any known rules of business. If the renowned physicist, Albert Einstein, had been a deejay, he might have suggested the theory that Radio was the "black hole" of all media, slowing sucking in any vestige of common sense.

So, it seemed the station I was about to start working for was basically on life-support and RKO was ready to pull the plug as soon as it found a buyer. This was a truly unfortunate circumstance for such a legendary company. At the beginning of each of its "Radio Pictures" it always featured the graphic of the now famous RKO radio tower beacon, emanating radio waves across the screen. In my mind, this was the company I was working for. In reality, it was a giant that had been slain by the F.C.C. The body was just still a little warm.

The day I arrived in Chicago was both exciting and daunting. I located the temporary apartment which the station had arranged for me and hauled my belongings up to it as quickly as possible. They agreed to put me up for three months. Being alone, I had no alternative but to leave my truck on the street, unattended, while I moved my belongings by elevator into my flat. I was sure half of it would be stolen between trips. My paranoia was unfounded and when I was finished, I stopped to look out my new front window which faced Michigan Avenue and surveyed a skyline chiseled by skyscrapers to my left, Grant Park in front of me and Lake Shore Drive behind it.

I was exhilarated and content. This was everything I had worked for my entire career. I was in the third largest market in America about to be on the air in a few days. I felt I had made it. I don't believe I will every feel quite like that again. I thought about those people I had met along the way who, for whatever personal reasons, were hoping I would fail. I wished I had a way to show them the view I was admiring.

In Radio, you learn to live with an endless stream of people who are motivated by jealousy and ego. And the bigger the market you work in, the more intense the disdain from your competitors - inside and outside the station you work. The afternoon guy wants to be the morning guy. The evening guy wants to be the afternoon guy. The unemployed guy wants to have any of their jobs. The guy in the smaller market wants the guy's job in the larger market. The guy competing against you cross-town wants you to die, or get picked up for drunk driving, or arrested for corrupting the morals of a 13-year-old girl. Anything to see you fail. Anything to get you out of town. Anything to get rid of you. Anything to get your job. It never ends.

Sometimes you feel like you're trying to race up a mountain of loose stones that keep slipping under your feet, all the while the people on each side of you are hoping you'll fall flat on your face and slide back down. I have known people I could swear were great friends - even close confidants - who later and quite suddenly turned on me, without provocation, to stab me in the back. Everyone in Radio has at one time been bad-mouthed, put down and lined up for character assassination and target practice. You get used to it and expect it.

I thought about all those people who had gunned for me and how badly I felt at the time. Now, I was finally able to let go of it. It was my turn to be vindicated. I had done what few in my business can or will do. In Radio, your market size is the stripes on your uniform and the medals on your chest.

I had been decorated, and highly.

I was also grateful. Some wonderful people had helped me along the way and I did not forget them. Specifically one man. On my trip to Illinois, I passed through Ohio. When I neared Newark, Ohio, I exited the highway. I traveled north on Route 13 one more time and turned into the parking lot of WCLT-AM/FM. I went to the back door and knocked on it. It was Saturday, but I was pretty certain the man I was looking for would be there working hard. The door opened and Bob Pricer stood there.

"Hello Mr. Pricer," I said. "Do you remember me?"

"Yes," he replied with a smile. "Corey. Corey Deitz! Come in!"

He escorted me to his office and we sat down. I told him I was on my way to Chicago to take a new job. His face lit up. I could see he was pleased. Bob Pricer gave much to radio
over the years. He allowed people like me to learn it, and helped us move on when we were ready.

"I would not be on this trip today" I said, "if it had not been for the kindness of people like you who helped me during those early years. I just wanted to stop by and say thank you."

He didn't speak for a moment. I could see he was genuinely touched. A certain contentment enveloped his face as if everything he had ever done was suddenly put very neatly in place. It meant a lot that I remembered him. Maybe that's all any of us strive for - to be remembered. The Bob Pricers and the Henry Del Toros - they all just want to be remembered.

We all just want to be remembered.

Sometimes, people mistakenly think their lives have not mattered much and then they are suddenly proven quite wrong. Bob Pricer spent his whole life in one of the smallest radio markets in America. Yet, his accomplishments were much worthier than any of my major market goals. I don't know if anyone else ever came back to thank him. If they didn't, they should have.

It's about personal validation.

We chatted for a while and then I said farewell. He wished me luck. I didn't think I would ever see him again, but I knew I had done the right thing. As it turns out, he died a few years later. But, he left a lot of himself in many people, including me. If I'm lucky, maybe someday I will have done some good for someone else and they will feel inspired enough to stop on their journey and thank me for a contribution of knowledge, advice or friendship.

That wouldn't be so bad.

Chicago was an extraordinary experience. Unfortunately, I spent the first 6 months there by myself, waiting for my wife to sell our home and then join me with the boys. My first night in town, Dick Rakovan, the General Manager, took me out to dinner. He brought me to an Italian restaurant called Gino & Georgetti's. He told me it was a place where you could see both "judges and mafia guys" having dinner together.

A deep fragrance of fresh tomato sauce filled the cigar-flavored air and Italian bread was carefully placed in the center of each table. It was busy with waiters quickly stepping back-and-forth between the kitchen and their assigned tables. The room buzzed with a mix of English and Italian conversation. If Al Capone were still alive, he'd be walking towards the table on my left, having just palmed a large tip to the maitre d'hotel.

This was the Chicago I had read about in books.

The next day, I left my apartment and walked north on Michigan Avenue toward the Prudential Building, where WFYR-FM was located. On top of the structure, a large white antenna reached into the sky. I stopped for a moment and stared at it. A slow panic began to consume me. I suddenly realized in just days, I would be pushing my voice through that big stick. It is very easy to feel insecure and inadequate when you are about to work in the same city where brilliant talents like Steve Dahl, Garry Meier, Jonathon Brandmeier, Fred Winston, Larry Lujack, John "Records" Landecker and so many more legendary talents have spent time.

I used the next week to try to psyche myself out of be psyched out.

Meanwhile, back in Virginia, my lawyer was still sparring verbally with the RKO attorneys. You'd think they would have been exhausted from their other legal troubles and ready to give in on any incomplete clause. But, there were still a few issues unresolved: I wanted to own the rights to anything I created, I wanted indemnity against lawsuits for content I had approved by the program director - a direct reaction to the lawsuit filed against me by the Virginia Beach judge - and my attorney wanted it to be a "no cut" contract. In other words, they payed me whether I worked or not, per their choice.

It came down to minutes.

Literally.

Minutes before I was supposed to do my first air-shift, the final version of my contract was faxed to WFYR's offices and Dick Rakovan and I executed the deal.

I walked down the hall and went into the on-air studio. A blended mixture of female and male voices in the top-of-the-hour jingle sang, "WFYR, Chicago!!!" and I punched up the next song.

I was now a Chicago radio personality and I was petrified.

But, at the same time I was exhilarated. I felt like Leonardo DiCaprio's character, Jack Dawson, in the movie *Titanic* when he stands on the bow of the doomed ocean liner and shouts out, "I'm king of the world."

As my voice reverberated across every street and into every alley of the nation's third largest radio market, I was not aware I was now broadcasting on a doomed ship that fate had already determined would soon sink.

But, the band played on a little longer.

On my first day, my immediate goal was simple: not to stumble over any words. Just as wild animals can sense fear in their prey, I was convinced any verbal misstep would leave me a marked man. I didn't even care if I wasn't very funny or entertaining that first day. I just didn't want to sound like I didn't belong in that city. College football coach Lou Holtz once said, "When you get to the end zone, act like you've been there before". I especially wanted whoever was listening to think I had been there before. Or at least that I belonged there.

Somehow, I survived my first 4 hours on the air. I'm sure it was adequate. Anyone in Radio knows it takes a week or two for an air-personality to become comfortable at a new job. The studio controls are new, the call letters, the phrases, the slogans, everything. It was also a big adjustment because for the first time in years I was now working without a partner. That did take some getting used to.

When you have a partner, you only have to worry about failing 50% of the time. But, by yourself, you are solely responsible for your show. Partners are good crutches you can lean on. It took some time to become truly confident and comfortable with just me again.

The other personalities at WFYR were great guys. Bob Barnes-Watts was the midday DJ. He was a British transplant who had been with the station about five years. Bob was easy going and didn't seem to take things too seriously. The guy who followed me, the evening jock, was "Smokin'" Joe Dawson. Joe was a great jock who seemed to know just about everybody else in radio. One of his buddies was the legendary Howard Hoffman who worked at WPIX-FM and WABC-AM in New York as well as a laundry list of other great markets like San Francisco, Houston, Phoenix and even Chicago. Back in 1974, Hoffman, along with Randy West, Russ DiBello and Pete Salant created a parody called *Nine! The Ultimate Radio Format.* It is now considered probably the best parody of the music radio format ever done.

The first time I met Howard, he was between jobs and living off the rest of a payed-off "no cut" contract. He said he just came to Chicago to hang out for a while with Joe. Occasionally, Howard would come up during his air-shift and the two of them would simply screw around. Howard would place fake calls to Joe's show and it was hysterical. He was one of the funniest ad-lib and voice talents I ever heard. At this writing, Howard is the Production Director for Disney's ABC Radio properties in Los Angeles including KABC Radio. He also is a very successful voice-overs artist for characters, animation, commercials and other multimedia.

Chicago is a great place to work because everybody pays attention to you: event promoters, networks, film companies, talent agents, record reps, and anyone else who has a product, service or client to promote. They all want you to mention their new TV show, new movie, new whatever. Actors, celebrities and interesting personalities are always available to the media there.

I interviewed guests like actors George Peppard and Hal Linden, and Improv founder Bud Friedman. I was visited by '60s and '70s bands like *"hree Dog Nigh"*, *Tommy James and the Shondells*, and *The Buckinghams*. A stream of comedians came through the studio like Redd Foxx, Jimmy Walker, Judy Tenuta, Soupy Sales, Michael Winslow (that guy from the Police Academy movies who does all the sound effects), Nora Dunn and Bobcat Goldthwaite.

Bobcat Goldthwaite. What a trip this guy was. *Police Academy 4 Citizens on Patrol* had been recently released. He was in town to promote the movie when somebody had the bright idea to put the both of us in one of the street-level display windows of the Marshall Fields department store on Michigan Avenue for a remote broadcast. So, for two hours one day, I attempted to do my show as Goldthwaite went bananas with fellow *Police Academy* actor Tim Kazurinsky. I loved Goldthwaite's humor but it was literally like being caged up with two crazed monkeys. Yes, you had great access to people in Chicago. I didn't say it always was a good thing.

There's a down side to having great celebrity interviews. Sometimes they don't want to be in your studio but are forced to by an agent or publicity firm in order to promote their new book, new film, or upcoming appearance. Other times they are tired, or bored, menstruating, or not feeling well or just sick of stupid questions by deejays. As a result, you get one-word answers, little enthusiasm, little eye contact and certainly no courtesy.

One afternoon, Dennis Miller was ushered into my show to promote his appearance in town that evening. The interview was going badly. He was bored, uninterested and not holding up his end of it. An interviewee who wants to promote something has an obligation to work with the interviewer. But, this was not happening. I was becoming annoyed because he was wasting my time and the whole segment just sucked. Finally, I said to him, "Look, if you don't want to be here, don't be here." He immediately got up and walked out. I apologized to the listeners for wasting their time and moved on.

Shit happens.

My Program Director, John Wetherbee, was one of the most supportive Program Directors I ever worked with. He was a friendly, gentle man who had the best intentions. John had been a jock during the WFYR glory days and now he was back for a second run at it, only this time in charge. He genuinely loved that radio station. I can't say one bad thing about the guy. He always had my back, defended my actions, and spoke well of me.

Walt Sabo was RKO's radio consultant. Walt would waltz in every month and do what consultants are supposed to do: observe, comment, suggest and in our case piss off the Program Director. There was a certain amount of tension between Wetherbee and Sabo. Maybe it was just Wetherbee protecting his territory or maybe there was something else between these two guys. Walt would inevitably want to sit down with me and talk about the show. Wetherbee would tell me to be nice and listen. There were no suggestion to actually abide by anything I was told.

This is the nature of consultants and Program Directors. They operate similarly to the Executive and Judicial branches of government. The consultant looks, listens and then judges but in most cases, it's the Program Director who actually executes the orders. And there's no guarantee those orders will be based on anything the consultant suggests. There's a remarkable "separation of powers" between the two.

Although I admired Wetherbee, I felt a small sense of loyalty to Sabo, too, as he had discovered me in Hampton Roads and recommended me for the Chicago job. Therefore, I listened to whatever he had to say, maybe more out of respect than loyalty. We would sit down and he would throw out interesting and sometimes bizarre ideas. I guess that's what a consultant is supposed to do.

What you have to understand about all consultants in any business is that they thrive where there is failure. Let's say your station is diving in the ratings and you hire a consultant. If he's pretty sharp and his advice helps to turn things around, the more successful the station becomes, the less it needs the consultant. This inverse ratio is not economically advantageous to a consultant. So, some convince the Program Director or

General Manager that they must be retained to nitpick to a point of absurdity with the ultimate goal of driving everybody nuts, especially the air-staff. I have known many consultants and it seems none of them agree on anything. Therefore, which one is right? Fuck, I don't know.

I think the real problem at WFYR was the ever-present shadow of the Grim Radio Reaper who hovered over RKO's corporate offices and our station. We were all treading water trying to make it look like our hopes were high and a rescue party would be along any moment. But, the sharks were near. We could feel them. It was just a matter of time before the station was sold.

Despite what loomed nearby, working in Chicago was great fun. I was offered great opportunities some people would give their right arm for which in some cases would make them qualified to run a station in Lewisburg, Pennsylvania. One night I was asked to represent the station at Comiskey Park where I threw the first pitch out during a game between the White Sox and The Boston Red Sox. Now there's a perk you won't get in too many jobs. On March 17, the staff rode an antique "'FYR-engine" in the St. Patrick's Day parade, waving to listeners as we snaked our way through the heart of the city. St. Patty's Day could only be better in Ireland, itself.

Being new to Chicago, I used my ability to create parody songs in pursuit of publicity. I wrote parody songs about every newsmaker and every situation. It got me some press and definitely got me noticed. One song actually almost interfered with the court system, itself. In his Radio/TV column, Robert Feder from the Chicago Sun Times reported:

Jurors in the Operation Incubator trial of Morgan M Finley and Clarence McClain were told not to listen to WFYR-FM (103.5) morning man Corey Deitz, A defense attorney feared some of Deitz's topical song parodies - such as "Dueling Bribes" and "You Used To Give Me Your Money" - might prejudice the jury.

Morning man?

Yes.

A series of changes occurred within the first year of my tenure at WFYR-FM. General Manager, Dick Rakovan, who never sold his home back east nor moved his wife to the Midwest, decided it was time to bail. He must have either always known he was a short-timer or the font of the writing on the wall suddenly became larger. He was replaced by Drew Horowitz, a well-known Chicago broadcast professional.

Next, Wetherbee was canned and Kenny Lee became the Program Director.

Finally, Larry Dixon, our morning guy, asked to be let out of his contract after 13 months. He and his wife just were not happy in Chicago and they wanted desperately to get out. It was a tough town to crack and he suddenly regretted leaving Dallas where he had spent many years building a good name for himself. Wetherbee resurfaced at WAGQ, Athens, Georgia and Dixon soon joined him there and eventually worked his way back to Dallas. The WFYR morning show had been and continued to be a revolving door.

When Dixon left - quite suddenly - I was offered the morning slot. I agreed on a raise which brought my salary up to a little over $120,000-a-year and my contract was redrawn. Of course, I had wanted to do mornings from the beginning and now I felt I would have the chance I needed. Unfortunately, only a few months went by before the plague, which had been slowly killing the RKO properties, finally caught up with WFYR-FM.

In a letter dated June 26, 1989, Pat Servodidio, President of RKO General wrote:

As you already know, the ownership of WFYR will be transferred from RKO to Summit Broadcast today. RKO and the station have been though a very trying period and I know that the last two years have been especially difficult for you. During that time, however, each of you at WFYR has maintained a commitment and spirit of which we are very proud.

It was over. On my last paycheck issued from RKO, the pay stub simply said, *"Happy Trails from RKO General, Thank You All!"* We had a big "Farewell, RKO - Hello, Summit!" dinner party where people were roasted, cocktails were poured, a slide show of memories was viewed and we all quietly mulled over our future.

Summit Communications, based in Atlanta, wasn't a terribly large company. They owned 16 stations and 4 cable systems and felt pretty good about themselves for plunking down $21 million dollars for WFYR-FM, which at the time was their biggest property. The first thing they did was come into town and have a big meeting where someone announced *"We're not buying a radio station, we're buying the people."*

I can guarantee you, if you ever hear that line from management, bend over and kiss your ass goodbye.

The second thing Summit did was fire Drew Horowitz, the General Manager, and replace him with Kelly Seaton. The first thing Kelly Seaton did was fire several more people, including me. Robert Feder, in the Chicago Sun-Times reported:

In a surprise round of firings at WFYR-FM (103.5) Monday, morning man Corey Deitz, midday man Bob Barnes-Watts, program director Kenny Lee and afternoon producer Diana Bodkins Yaccino were dropped from the oldies station. No permanent replacements were named. WFYR general manager Kelly Seaton said the moves were recommended by a program consultant for Atlanta-based Summit Broadcasting... "We'll be taking a slight shift in direction within the oldies genre," Seaton said. Deitz, who joined the station 16 months ago, and Barnes-Watts, a five-year "FYR veteran, were paid off for the remainder of their contracts.

The morning I was fired, I got off the air and was asked to come to the General Manager's office. I went in and Kelly Seaton said to me, "Your services are no longer required." Then she handed me a check for $80,000 dollars.

$80-thousand-fucking-dollars!

I had struck it rich and won the *GET OUT YOU'RE FIRED* Lottery!

Didn't I tell you in the beginning that this business pays people for not working?

Now, think about this for just a moment. You're a company and you have a contract to pay someone another $80 grand. Wouldn't it make just a little more sense to sit down with the guy and say, "Hey...we're gonna' change things up around here. Let's talk about another place with the company where we could both benefit." Yeah, I know how reasonable that sounds.

But, upstart radio companies who run into the "end zone" - having never been there before - usually wind up trying to demonstrate how big their balls are by throwing money around. Indiscriminately. It's the all-time "Great Gonad Bluff" play. Make 'em think you've got so much in resources, you can piss Ben Franklins as long as need be in order to get what you want.

But, the decision had been made and I would have given anything to stay. I loved Chicago and I loved WFYR-FM. The money didn't mean a thing to me. I would have given the check back without hesitation if it would have changed what had just occurred.

I was speechless. I really was. I looked at her, looked at the check and tried very quickly to make sense of it all. I had a lot of money in my palm. I suppose I could have considered it due payment for all the years I had jumped from one market to another, one job to another, one studio to another, one cash cage to another - just to get ahead. After all, I had made those choices, consciously, yet now the money was so unfulfilling. I thought Summit would be a new beginning. But for me, and others, it was a sudden ending. They wanted me out right away. Get your stuff, give us your building pass, thanks a lot and please leave.

In Radio, they always do that to you when you are fired. I guess they're afraid you'll do something sudden and terrible like - try to say goodbye to people who you've worked with while still maintaining your dignity. After all, we can't have that. What if everyone started insisting on his or her dignity? It would be anarchy!

When you're fired in Radio, you suddenly are morphed into deadly bacteria. It's extremely important that the station cleanse and extract you from the environment so you don't have a chance to infect anyone or take anyone else down with you. Management types are highly fearful that the fired person will say something negative and that, in itself, will force a spontaneous stampede of resignations from people who just needed one more comment to throw them into an utter fit of upheaval.

Ironically, the day before my contract was payed off, my wife Chris and I had been shopping at Water Tower, a mall on Michigan Avenue. We walked into a jewelry store and she spotted some piece she liked that was maybe $300 or $400 dollars. I said to her, "Buy it. We can finally afford it. I make $120,000-a-year."

Little did I know that would be the last time I would be able to say that.

I went home, walked in the front door and said to my wife, "I have some good news and some bad news." I showed her the check and said,

"The bad news is I've been fired." We were both pretty sullen and it took us a few days to digest everything. What kept going through my head was this: how bad could I be that someone would be willing to pay me $80,000 to not perform? Of course, I was personalizing it to a point of ridiculous self-destruction. It wasn't that at all.

WFYR-FM had been dying for a long time. Instead of assessing its resources carefully, Summit just decided to blow it up and start over. As luck would have it, I was part of the first volley of firings as ordained by the Summit consultant. There was a second round of firings soon after and eventually, the whole format was changed and new blood was infused into the air-staff. This behavior is more common in Radio than unshaven morning men are.

If my lawyer had not protected me with the "no cut" clause in my contract, I would have been out in the street with practically nothing. Instead, the money Summit was legally obligated to give me for the privilege of going away, turned out to be the funds my wife and I eventually used to finally move up in the housing market. It also allowed us to begin a retirement savings plan.

In retrospect, getting payed off wasn't so bad.

At least Howard Hoffman would have been proud.

Chapter 14

The only thing that made me feel a little better about getting fired was that in the same month I was let go, it seems everyone in Chicago radio was being axed. Fred Winston was given his walking papers at WLS-AM after 6 years and wound up at WFYR-FM's oldies competitor, WMJK-FM where he replaced Tommy Edwards. Morning man Paul Barskey was fired at WYTZ-FM, a CHR outlet. Pete Stacker was tossed out at Adult Contemporary WTMX-FM.

I didn't apply for unemployment at first. As a matter of fact, I waited three months. I suppose I was in denial. Plus, I figured what difference did it make? I had just deposited a check at the bank for over $80,000 dollars, minus taxes, and didn't figure to be in immediate financial jeopardy.

I knew I was in a difficult situation, though. I had been riding a wave of continual progress for five years in both market size and salary. Where exactly could I go from here, the third largest market in America, making over $120,000-a-year? How many jobs were really at that level and above? If I wanted to maintain major market status and a paycheck to reflect that, I was severely limited in what was available. What's worse, stations in smaller markets would look at my credentials and salary history and decide I was out of their price range.

In a way, I sabotaged my career with my own success. The higher you climb, the harder you hit on the way down.

The irony is if I had been less of an achiever, I would have been more employable at this point. Now, though, I had much to lose. I had finally tasted the sweetness of being able to make enough money so as not to have to worry about making enough money. Or at least I thought I did. In reality, I had made the classic mistake thinking the more money I made, the more freedom it afforded me.

It doesn't matter how much money you earn *if* it comes at the expense of working for someone else. This is far from any path of personal freedom because in exchange for the cash, you hand over control of your life to the people paying you. You subjugate your life to the process itself. The money brings you possessions, expensive dinners, and even spontaneous gifts. Then, suddenly, you like it too much and think you must always live this way. You panic and desperately wonder how you will keep the big bucks coming in.

Currency becomes a drug.

You are mainlining dollars.

You are addicted.

This was the lure of the cash cage I had readily stepped into. The lyrics in *"Hotel California"* by the Eagles say it all:

You can check out any time you like

But you can never leave

I devoted part of each day of my unemployment to the job search. Other than that, I was so disappointed, so sad, so disheartened about losing the Chicago gig; I didn't care about much else. In my mind, I was a failure and I was very hard on myself.

In retrospect, what I should have done was taken a month long road trip out west. The kind of road trip where you see uplifting visuals like dead armadillos and steer horns on the side of the road. Nothing makes you want for the great outdoors like being locked up in a radio studio every day.

I should have sought out the sweet smell of a cheeseburger being served up in a diner that appears to be shaped like a flying saucer. This is the America I'm talking about! Nothing says unemployment like waking up in the morning, curled up on the front seat of your car, being eyed by a buzzard that is carefully perched on a cactus and leering at the half-eaten Clark bar on your dashboard.

Yes, unemployment is wasted on too many concerned job hunters who just can't appreciate the freedom of being broke.

About three months into my job search, I received a call from a man named Robert Hyland. He was calling from St. Louis, the country's 20th largest radio market, and wanted to talk to me about a job opening at an Oldies station called KLOU-FM. We arranged an interview and a few days later, I flew into town and we met. Robert Hyland, when he was alive, was an enigma. He died in 1992 but up until his death, he was probably the most respected man in the CBS Radio Division and the second most respected person in all of CBS, next to founder, William Paley.

People seemed just plain scared of Robert Hyland. It wasn't that he was a mean man, or unfair or even unlikable. But, he was a brooding personality who was so much larger than life; you naturally stepped back and let him pass by when he walked down the hallway. I always had the impression people who worked for him would have felt more comfortable being permitted to bow upon entering and leaving his presence. But, I'm sure there was something in the CBS employee manual that forbade such actions.

Robert Hyland started with CBS radio in 1950 at WBBM-AM in Chicago. A couple of years later, he returned to his home, St. Louis, and took over the now legendary KMOX-AM. He did well as Sales Manager and by 1955 became General Manager. He held that position until his death. KMOX was a CBS owned-and-operated property and under Hyland, it consistently had the highest grossing revenues in the CBS Radio chain, along with the highest listener ratings. How did he do this?

Beginning in 1960 (by one account), he pointed KMOX in a new direction: Talk. Hyland is actually credited with inventing the format. Under his guidance, KMOX became the first major radio station to successfully do an all-talk format. He called it "*At Your Service*". KMOX also became known for its sports programming featuring the St. Louis Cardinals and other local teams. In 1962, CBS purchased a St. Louis FM frequency that became KMOX-FM. It was later renamed KLOU-FM, the station Hyland was now restocking with talent.

The "*House that Hyland Built*" was an extraordinary operation. When I had occasion to be in the KMOX studios for some production purposes or other reasons, it was always a treat. The first time I was there, I was introduced to Art Fleming, best known as the original host to the television show "Jeopardy" from 1964 to 1978.

When I met him, Fleming was hosting a midday show on KMOX. Later I got to know famed sportscaster, Jack Buck, who was usually walking through the halls, preparing for a St. Louis Cardinals game, his own show, or readying himself to leave town to do a national broadcast for CBS Sports. Then there was Bob Costas. Costas began at KMOX in 1978 and joined CBS Sports in 1979. He shuttled back and forth providing services to both, maintaining his home in St. Louis. Bob Costas was spoken of with the reverence of a deity and whenever it was known he was returning to KMOX for whatever reason, the place was giddy with excitement. There was no doubt, he had made everyone proud.

With the kind of talent Robert Hyland had nurtured, he was easily thought of as a kingmaker. He was powerful and could make or break people. But, it wasn't so much the absolute achievements of Hyland, the tales from his employees, or even the unwavering success of KMOX that created the man's mystique. The fact is he was a notorious workaholic.

Sometimes, when I would arrive at KLOU-FM between 2 and 3 a.m., Hyland would already be there, getting on the elevator with me! His long work hours were legendary and unheard of for a manager. Based on his work ethic and successes, William Paley once offered Hyland the job as head of CBS Sports and later as head of CBS Radio Network, but Hyland declined. He liked living and working in St. Louis.

Robert Hyland was a classy man, too. On holidays, he was known to send up food platters from a caterer for any staff members who pulled the short straw for that day. He gave back respect in the same way it was shown to him.

When I arrived to first meet Robert Hyland, I did not know any of what I just told you. I only knew he had a job open at this FM oldies station and to me, St. Louis was a respectable place for me to land after Chicago.

The interview went well, at least well enough for him to offer me a job at the end of it. Somewhere in the middle, the Program Director was ushered in to join us, but it was Hyland making the decisions. Then, he asked me how much salary I needed, which is always a loaded question. I was unemployed and did not have much bargaining power. I knew I was not going to be earning my Chicago salary and he knew he probably could not afford to pay it, either. I think I countered his question with something generic like "...a reasonable salary" and threw it back in his lap.

He thought for a moment and said, "$80,000".

"Hell," I thought to myself, "I make $80,000 just getting fired these days."

Considering the circumstances, though, I was pleased. I just wanted to get back to work. No contract was signed and I don't recall whether we even discussed one. For some reason, it didn't seem to matter to him nor me. Robert Hyland was a man of his word and I suppose he sensed I was, too. Things worked a little differently in St. Louis than Chicago. We agreed I would start within two weeks.

Oh, there was one more thing. My name. Hyland did not like my last name.

"Deitz," he said. "It sounds like ditz. I don't want people thinking you're a ditz."

I thought this was pretty fucking stupid. I had been pronouncing my name for decades, ever since I was a small child in New Jersey. Not once did I ever say "Hi, I'm Corey Ditz. Oops! I mean Deitz! Deitz! Sorry! I don't know what the fuck came over me! Deitz! Jesus! Deitz! Not Ditz! Deitz!"

Although not as prevalent today, there was a time when most deejays had fake names. I suppose one might defend the practice as being important to the total package of entertainment. For instance, the night jock on a CHR station is going to attract more 13-year-olds with a name like "Surf Dude" than by using his real name, "Marvin Elroy Dorfmeister".

Some argue a fake name protects the person on the air from undue harassment, especially those who do controversial shows. Still, other jocks no doubt found phony names useful because it made it harder for 16-year-olds to find their home phone number after a night of jailbait sex.

There's an industry inside joke about how most deejay names usually consist of two first names. I call it the "Rule of Two". For instance: John Barry, Jeff Morgan, and John Lawrence were three guys I worked with at Q94 in Richmond. All first names.

Even though I disagreed on the name change, Hyland's mind was made up. I wasn't really in a position to argue. So, we sat there and started throwing new ones around. Finally, he said, "Roberts".

"Corey Roberts"

I reluctantly agreed. Is it any wonder my last name was really a derivative of his first name? Everything at the CBS operations in St. Louis revolved around Robert Hyland.

We shook hands and I departed.

As usual, I moved ahead of my wife, Chris, who hung back to sell our home in Westmont, the Chicago suburb where we had been living. Hyland put me up in a downtown hotel for 3 months while Chris and I waited for construction to finish on a new home we purchased, courtesy of my former employer, Summit Broadcasting. In the meantime, I ordered room service almost every night and charged it to the station: Pizza, chocolate cake and coffee.

The reason I had been offered the afternoon slot at KLOU-FM and not mornings was because John "Records" Landecker was supposed to be the new morning man. All preparations were being made to welcome Landecker to St. Louis. The story I was told was simply that it was pretty much a done deal. At least Robert Hyland thought it was. So, I arrived when I said I would and hit the air a couple of days later. Hyland seemed pleased with my initial performance.

During my first week on the air, one afternoon he strolled into the studio and we chatted briefly. No matter what anyone said, and despite General Managers and Program Directors, it was Hyland who really ran both KMOX-AM and KLOU-FM with his unique hands-on approach. Maybe it was more like a grip. I sensed he liked me a lot. He spoke positively of the opportunities ahead with the company. As he left the studio, he said to me was "Ya know, this ain't no cup of coffee."

A funny thing to say, I thought to myself. It turned out the CBS operations in St. Louis were more like a "Tempest in a Teacup". A tempest is a violent commotion or disturbance. Put that in a teacup and you're looking at instability on a grand scale. The big problem at these two stations was the incessant political maneuvering people spent most of their time worrying about. I think it was simply that Hyland's work ethic was so extraordinary, nobody measured up, period. The best anyone could do was cover his or her ass from 8 a.m. until 5 p.m.

Meanwhile, the countdown to Landecker was proceeding on schedule. But, then, on the Friday before the Monday of his debut, I was summoned to Hyland's office where the news was regretfully disclosed: no Landecker.

The specifics were not discussed. It was simply stated that Landecker would not be the new morning man at KLOU-FM. He had changed his mind and was staying in Chicago. I couldn't blame him. As to why, I can only speculate. My gut tells me he probably did work a deal with Hyland but delayed signing any contract in the hopes of still landing a new gig in his beloved Chicago. I imagine Hyland must have taken this news badly, especially after what must have been lengthy negotiations and concessions. Robert Hyland liked getting his way and Landecker bailing out like this was akin to treason.

I, too, was disappointed Landecker would not be coming to St. Louis. After all, he was on my short list of Radio heroes. But, his absence just created a new opportunity and Hyland offered the morning slot to me. Of course, I agreed immediately and reassured him I could do a great job.

I mentioned a raise. He acknowledged my mention. We were supposed to talk later and I said "sure" because I was a team player.

Warning: team players often get lost in the shuffle because they are so reliable the people whose asses they're covering usually forget they are even there. My advice to you no matter what your job: be courteous, display your talent, work hard but never confuse being "a team player" with being firm about your expectations for compensation.

I never received that raise and was a little miffed only out of principle because the subject was never broached again. It wasn't so much the money as it was the issue of personal dignity. I respect commitments and if you say we'll "talk later", I expect us to have that chat. And I also expect the person who proposed it, to take the initiative to make it happen. I don't want to have to keep pestering someone to make good on his or her own word. That's demeaning and humiliating.

I was teamed up with a new sidekick, Brian Kirchoff, a nice enough guy who had been doing some part-time work for the station. Kathe Hartley, from KMOX, was designated our newswoman and suddenly a new morning show was born. The program director wanted to know what we were going to call it and we ran through a litany of possibilities:

"Corey and Brian in the Morning"

"The Morning Show with Corey and Brian"

"Corey Roberts and Friends"

"Roberts and Friends with Corey and Brian"

"Roberts, Friends, Corey, Brian *and* a Psychotic Program Director" (Personally, my favorite choice but I'll come back to this in a moment.)

In the end, I was staring at one of the comedy services the station was subscribed to called "Morning Circus" and I said, "How about the 'KLOU 103 Morning Circus"?

I regretted even suggesting it. The moment the words left my lips I cringed. But, it was too late. The Program Director liked it. And so it was. We named the new morning show after a stupid comedy service.

Anyway, this was insignificant next to the series of events that began to unfold. While I was still doing afternoons, everyone loved me. It seemed I could do no wrong. I was a golden boy. But, the following Monday - after just signing on as the new KLOU morning man - everything changed.

I hadn't been on the air more than ten minutes when I executed the mechanics of a new contest exactly as earlier instructed. The hotline rang immediately and the Program Director launched into a tirade of curse words the likes I had never heard from management. Whatever set him off, he never quite explained since there wasn't enough space in between his monologue of obscenities.

Somewhere between Friday and Monday, this guy had turned into the scariest, craziest son-of-a-bitch I ever met.

I can offer you no explanation or reason for this outrageous outburst except to suggest the Program Director's behavior toward me morphed from what earlier appeared to have been a normal person (as normal as you can be in Radio) into a raving psychotic. I can't stress enough how much I believe this man needed a strait jacket.

All of the employees under him should have been issued regulation CBS dart guns, with the tips dipped in some kind of sedative. He needed a full-blown, funny Pope Hat, Vatican-endorsed exorcism. In Virginia Beach I was convinced my partner was Satan. In St. Louis, my Program Director seemed to be possessed by him.

Here it was just a few weeks into my new job and I knew I was fucked...again. I tried to blow it off and forget it but my instincts kept pounding my brain, warning me that I had stepped into Radio's mental ward.

The Program Director never regained that nice composure he demonstrated prior to my switch to mornings. Whoever *that* guy was, he left and never came back. He had officially become Radio's Dr. Jekyl and

Mr. Hyde. All of a sudden, I was working for someone whose actions toward me seemed not only unstable, but also clearly dangerous. But, I was stuck. The house my wife and I were building was just about finished and even though I didn't have a contract with the station, I did have a very large financial commitment and deposit in this new home. I figured, I would stick it out and hope things changed.

They didn't.

I attended countless post-show meetings over an endless array of stupid and minor issues which only an obsessive, micro-managing Program Director could devise. If there was a Radio Hell that deejays went to after they died, it was this guy's office.

For the next nine months, I carefully and delicately tiptoed around the station and when I was home, dreaded phone calls. My wife and I fully expected I would be fired the next time it rang. Things were that tense. CBS in St. Louis was a tie-wearing, cover-your-butt operation, of which I was doing both.

After the Program Director's behavior toward me went insane, I came to distrust him so much, I decided the only way I could protect myself was to maintain a diary of my daily interactions with him. So, I began to document our meetings and discussions, what he told me and how he said it. I wanted to make damn sure when the shit hit the fan, I had an explanation for why I did whatever it was he was insisting I do on and off the air.

The Program Director eventually did himself in. There's a thing called "contest fixing" and you don't do it because:

1) It's wrong and

2) It really pisses off the F.C.C.

When you give away a prize to the 12th caller or whoever you say is going to win it, that 12th caller gets it whether the caller is a he or a she, or is 18, 25, 45 or 70 years old -except if the contest rules specify an age limit. It's something called fairness. Well, what the Program Director really wanted to hear was the sound of somebody winning on the air that was in our demographic. So, he told me to pass over callers - even if they were the true winner - if they did not sound like our demo.

I protested.

He didn't care.

I wrote it down in my diary.

Somewhere into my nine months in St. Louis, the General Manager apparently became concerned about the Program Director or his performance. I'm not sure which. Maybe he spotted him one night naked and dancing around an alter, praying to the great Chipmunk God. Sure, I thought he was nuts but, the G.M. may have had his own reasons. Whatever they were, I'm sure it was also political because that was the nature of CBS Radio management in St. Louis.

It was obvious some heavy ass-covering was about to happen.

The General Manager began to psychologically put his arm around me and pick my brain about the Program Director until I was lulled into a sense of safety. I began to spill the beans. He was very interested in what I had to say and before it was all said and done, he had a copy of certain pages of my diary and The Program Director and I were sitting in the General Manager's office doing a he said/she said thing.

I kept thinking I was the "she" in this thing and in the end, I was going to get fucked.

I was petrified. It became increasingly apparent to me that I was in the middle of a process that would lead to Mr. Whack Job's dismissal and I was the star witness. Sure, I wanted the guy fired but I didn't want him to know I had anything to do with it. This is probably how Kato Kaelin felt when they asked him to testify against O.J. I'm sure he was thinking to himself, "Okay, I'll talk. You just make sure you get a conviction because if you don't, I'm gonna' to be looking over my shoulder for the rest of my life watching out for that son-of-a-bitch."

The Program Director was fired shortly thereafter and I was convinced he was going to gun me down. No, really. That's how disturbed I thought this guy was. I was so intimidated by this man's psychotic possibilities, for weeks I took different routes to and from work just in case he was stalking me. While driving, I was constantly looking in my rear-view mirror to see if I was being followed. I swear. I was afraid to answer my phone because I thought the next call would be him threatening my life.

I don't scare easily but the pattern of this guy's behavior gave me reason to worry. There were rumors prior to his dismissal that he had roughed up a former girlfriend who subsequently moved out and left him.

I felt he was prone to violence and as such, might direct some my way. I know it may sound silly, but I can assure you my fears were real and a direct reaction to the disturbing behavior the former Program Director exhibited over many months.

Contrary to what I thought would happen, the general working environment at KLOU-FM continued to degenerate. Even with this one cancer surgically removed, it was still not a very happy place. KLOU was not performing as well as management wanted so all conversations were laced with that unique, stressful anxiety you can feel when personnel changes are being considered. Thankfully, I only worked in St. Louis for nine months.

Then, one day Rita Bentley from Q94 in Richmond called me. Rita was still on the "Q Morning Zoo" and was feeling me out on behalf of her boss, Steve Davis. She wanted to know if I had any interest in returning to Richmond.

"Yes," I said. "Absolutely!"

I had my fill of CBS's tribal sacrificial mores and was still smarting from the Chicago firing. I was ready to vote myself off the island.

"Fuck this major market bullshit," I thought to myself.

At this point, the thought of finding some refuge in a medium market where the Program Director wasn't a serial killer seemed somewhat appealing. After a few weeks of negotiations, it was a done deal. I would return to Richmond and rejoin the morning show.

I handed in my notice at KLOU and hardly anyone blinked. It's as if they expected it at any moment.

After leaving St. Louis, I never heard another word about Psycho P.D. I'm sure he was killed by his own employees. Find him and you'll probably also find Jimmy Hoffa – and of course, Bob Canada, too.

The man who had brought me there, Robert Hyland, died two years later in 1992. That year CBS announced its intention to sell KLOU-FM.

So ended that lineage of the CBS dynasty.

Chapter 15

They say you can never go home. Not true. When I returned to Richmond in the fall of 1990, I felt like I had. If anywhere in the country felt like a home to me - besides Ohio - it was Virginia. I was returning to work with people who were in Radio for the right reasons. At least as far as I was concerned. I was working for Phil Goldman again, one of a handful of decent men I had known in the business. I was once again performing with the multi-talented Rita Bentley, the kind of person who makes everyone around her look good.

My new immediate superior was Steve Davis, and although I really didn't know him, Rita had vouched for his integrity and that was good enough for me. She had also vouched for me, so we were even in that respect. I was working again for the listeners of Q94, probably the most active and loyal fans I had encountered in my succession of moves around the country. And finally, I was working with someone completely new to me: Jay Hamilton.

Jay is the funniest person I've ever known. Nobody makes me laugh like Jay. During his job interview Phil Goldman asked, "Jay, how do you feel about a drug test?" and Jay responded calmly, "It depends on which ones you want me to try."

That's all Phil needed to hear. It clinched the job for Jay.

Jay had come to Q94 shortly before my return. He was hired to join Steve Davis on the morning show fresh from a stint with "The American Comedy Network" where he had spent the last couple of years as a producer for their syndicated weekly comedy service. At the time, ACN was the most respected comedy service in the country.

But, comedy is a bitch and the pressure of churning out a weekly menu of topical humor for hundreds of radio stations began to take its toll on Jay. He thought doing mornings in Richmond would be a good move. A few months after his arrival, Davis decided he needed to get out from under the responsibilities of being on the air to devote himself to other management duties. That's when my name came up again.

When Bob McNeil left the original Q-Zoo, it was tough on the show. Then, when I departed, the identity of the show began to dissolve even more. A revolving door of talent went through the anchor position between 1986 and 1990 and the morning show floundered. The idea of bringing me back was to recapture some of the original magic and Goldman, probably more than Davis, felt I was capable of doing it. That's why I was given a lot of leeway in how I wanted to conduct the show.

Part of the agreement I had with Davis and Goldman was that if I didn't get along with Jay, he would be replaced with someone of my liking. It was nothing against Jay, but the reality of the situation was Q94 needed to put itself back into the game so it was imperative to shore up the morning show and fast.

If it had not worked out between us, Jay would not have been fired. Phil Goldman did not operate that way. If Phil brought Jay down to Richmond and said he had a job, then he was not the type of man to pull the carpet out from underneath him after a few months. He'd sooner lay down, himself, so you could gently walk over him rather than let you fall. That's the type of man he was and that's why he inspired loyalty in everyone who worked for him.

As was our usual pattern, Chris stayed behind in St. Louis with the boys to sell the house. The station put me up for 2 months and then I had to strike out on my own. When I moved into a one-room efficiency I rented in the west end of Richmond, I did not realize I would wind up living in it for another 6 months. As it turned out, Saddam Hussein decided to invade Kuwait on August 2, 1990, a day or so after we put our St. Louis home up for sale.

I don't know whether you have ever owned your own home but there are three things you need to know when buying real estate:

1) Location
2) Location
3) ~~Location~~ No wars in the Middle East

Prospective homeowners are usually flexible about many things like interest rates or a little water under the house. But, when Arab dictators from third-world countries are threatening the "Mother of All Battles", this tends to put buyers off. Trust me on this.

Our house sat listless for 6 months. The initial threat of hostilities and then the Persian Gulf War itself kept everyone hunkered down. Our real estate agent was a waste of time and in the end, it was Chris who cut a deal with a buyer just so we could get out from underneath the payments. We took a $20,000 dollar loss. If it hadn't been part of the buy-out money from Chicago, it might have been more painful.

The only bad part about going back to Richmond was leaving my family behind.

Again.

In a sense, it was becoming a normal part of our lives for me to disappear for 3 or 6 months every few years. I arrived in Richmond in September and did not see Chris or the boys until Christmas. And that almost didn't happen. When I flew into St. Louis, Christmas Eve of 1990, a snowstorm was right on my heels. My plane was the last to be permitted to land at the St. Louis airport on December 24. Chris and the boys were there waiting and it was a sweet reunion. We drove home and that night, Missouri had a white Christmas. We spent the next week snowed in. It was a postcard holiday.

I was forced to fly back to Richmond on New Year's Eve. The only thing worse than being alone is being alone on a holiday. I knew the separation was slowly consuming my wife.

Chris is an extraordinary woman. Today, she is a nationally acclaimed educator who boasts many prestigious awards. She has been honored so many times, I can't even keep count. But, when kids came along, she set aside her professional goals to raise them. While the boys were growing up, she anchored our family during all our moves, sold the houses, nurtured the kids during my long absences and creatively solved a lot of problems because there was no one else there to do it.

We both agree genetics must have had something to do with why our marriage stayed intact all these years. Any other woman would have left me long ago because of the incessant moving. Not Chris. Somewhere, deep inside her DNA, are the genes of a nomad, a traveler, a wanderer. She has fortitude for new experiences and the unknown. There can be no other explanation.

The woman has U-Haul grease in her joints.

When the Persian Gulf War began on January 17, 1991, we were hundreds of miles apart and she was left alone, with no other family to help. Being at war is a chilling experience and the Persian Gulf battle was the first one to be broadcast on television in colorful green night-vision.

Live war in your family room can be disconcerting. I tried to comfort her as best I could, but, the strain of covering for me while I moved ahead each time finally caught up with her.

When the sale of the house eventually closed, my father-in-law had to travel from Cambridge, Ohio to St. Louis to drive his daughter and our babies to Richmond. By the time she joined me in Richmond in April of 1991, Chris was having a nervous breakdown.

By now, she had been dealing with 12 years of moving from place to place and each one just kept getting harder. The stress, the fatigue, the loneliness. Lesser women would have left someone like me long ago. Asking a woman to be a Radio wife is a lot and it probably explains why the divorce rate in this business is pretty high.

It took a long time for her to heal.

We rented a home for a year and during that time, purchased 10 acres of land in Beaverdam, Virginia, north of the city of Richmond. We soon built a slightly modified version of the home we had in St. Louis and moved in at the end of our lease. I had always wanted to live out in the country and Chris was finally at the point where she, too, just wanted to have her own space where there was no worry of anyone else's noise or nosiness.

Being in the country was glorious. The land we picked was once owned by the American patriot, Patrick Henry. It was a small parcel of 10 acres, at one time part of Henry's full estate that stretched out for hundreds of acres. Just up the road from us - maybe two miles - Patrick Henry's home, Scotchtown, still stood, now preserved and restored. Living on land he had once owned was a respectful experience. Not a week went by I didn't think about how Patrick Henry might have stood where I was standing, might have planted where I was digging, or might have gazed where I was looking. For all I knew, I was probably standing in Patrick Henry's garden.

To make our country living even sweeter, just a few miles in the opposite direction of Henry's home was the 203-acre Ashland Berry Farm. The Ashland Berry Farm is owned by Ken Gustafson who we first befriended when we lived in Richmond during the mid 1980s. His was a great story. One day Ken decided he wanted to be a farmer. So, he looked around until he found the right farm and in 1978 he purchased it. He began, knowing very little about it at first, but learned more each day. Ken built his own log cabin home on the farm and resurrected the fields one-by-one until it was a functioning business. Several restored barns and a silo overgrown by creeping foliage greeted you when you drove into the parking lot. It was a friendly place.

In June, people came from miles around to pick his strawberries. A tractor with a bed attached, carried pickers out to the fields and dropped them off. You picked as much as you wanted and in between, ate as much as you cared to off the strawberry bushes. When you were done, the tractor brought you back to the beginning where your strawberries were weighed and you settled up. There was no charge for the ones already being digested.

Chris and I used to take our boys to the Ashland Berry Farm and sit them down on the soft dirt in between the long rows of berry bushes to let them pick or eat their choice. My memories of their faces stained with strawberries are vividly framed against the warm afternoons in which they occurred.

Then, in the fall, when it was cooler, it became pumpkin-picking time. Tractors followed similar dirt routes and carried visitors out to the patches where you selected the perfect-sized and colored pumpkins for autumn decorating or October carving. You made sure to grab a lot, too, because at the Ashland Berry Farm, it was one price for all-you-could-carry. And you really did have to carry the pumpkins, at least for a few feet.

Once we got back to where the cashiers were, the family would stack the pumpkins on me in just the perfect balance so I could waddle across the line and claim them as ours. In October, there was always apple cider available for thirsty visitors, fresh and warm donuts plus a haunted house for the kids each Halloween.

I had always loved the Ashland Berry Farm and now, we were neighbors. To me, living this close to it was almost as good as owning it. I often fantasized about how wonderful that would be. I still do. Granted, I don't know the first thing about farming. But, if given the chance, I would try it in a heartbeat. I'm not even sure, myself, why I find it attractive. Maybe it's the simplicity. We can pretend to be sophisticated and civilized people with learned ways and wonderful technologies but at the end of the day, a man's instincts are pretty basic: to use his hands to alter something for the better, be it a screen door repair, splitting wood for a fireplace, seeding a field or welding beams for a skyscraper.

I don't need another computer or PDA or cell phone in my life.

What I need is the opportunity to work at something where I sweat hard enough to really deserve my next meal.

How better to appreciate what the world has to offer than to know the grace of that provided to us through the Creator by becoming personal with the process of survival. Most of us have jobs today that distance us from anything close to a basic instinct. We have been sanitized and cleansed.

When all is said and done, we are still really hunters and gatherers. It doesn't matter how many suits you wear or how much makeup you apply. Underneath it all, that is who we are.

But, I'm not a farmer, I'm a radio personality.

Jay and I had great success as we continued the tradition of the Q-Zoo at Q94.

Our target demo was women, 18-49 and we had a lot of fun achieving it. At that time, stunts were in vogue and we did a lot of them. Like the time we offered a prize to a lady for running over her cell phone so we could hear the connection go blank as her tire crushed it. We convinced another listener to wrap her telephone in a plastic bag, immerse it in oatmeal and try to still communicate with us by yelling into the boiling cereal. We found someone with a "Clapper" and remotely started a blender by having her hold the phone up to her radio as we clapped our hands. There was the guy we sent up onto a car roof in traffic who began driving eggs with a 3 wood.

Then there was the "Mail Us an Egg" contest. The rules were simple: package a raw egg against breakage and mail it to us. We would randomly pick an entry and open it. If the egg was unbroken, you won $500 dollars. I think close to 100 packages arrived, some rather soggy. The Postal Service was not pleased. As a matter of fact, it was downright pissed, especially when we followed up with the "Mail Us a Banana Contest"! I know it's hard to believe but people affixed postage to bananas and yes, the Postal Service - grudgingly - delivered them.

In a stunt called *"Bras Across the James"*, we collected hundreds of brassieres from women and strung them together in a line long enough to reach from one side of the James River to the other. Jay, Rita Bentley and other staff members in rowboats dragged the underwear slowly from one shore to the other while I anchored the event back in the studio. Nobody could have realized how heavy the material would become when wet. They barely made it. Minutes after reaching across, the line of bras snapped and sending a torrent of bras rushing downstream. It didn't matter. We were satisfied with the momentary and dubious accomplishment.

There have always been people, be them interns, devoted listeners who want to be part of a show, or other pliable bodies who are agreeable to doing stupid things upon request. In the 1990s, many radio shows had a "Danger Boy". We sent ours out on a number of dumb missions dressed in a very comic-book-like superhero costume.

Our Danger Boy even became ordained by a mail-order church so he could marry listeners. One couple stepped forward and happily volunteered to take their vows from our 19-year-old postal-approved minister. The wedding occurred live on the air one morning from outside our studios on Church Hill in downtown Richmond. The *Richmond Times Dispatch* reported:

Radio station Q-94, having bizarrely, successfully (and even somewhat tastefully) pulled off a 'Danger Wedding' on its Morning Zoo Friday.... Zoo character 'Danger Boy' ordained as a 'minister by mail' presided over a nearly legit, black-tie wedding...

Virginia Governor Doug Wilder probably could have done without us. When we couldn't get him to commit to coming on our show as a guest we gave out his office number on the air and asked listeners to call him on our behalf. Apparently his office received so many calls they began interfering with State business. He subsequently scheduled a visit to our show. Later, when the Governor was exploring the possibility of running for President of the United States, we disagreed thinking he needed to devote his time to Virginia, the job and responsibility he was put in office to do. We printed up and distributed bumper stickers that said "Wilder for Resident". He eventually elected not to run.

Then there was the alleged affair between the former beauty queen and the local news anchor. WRIC-TV's married news anchor, Kevin

McGraw was reported to be having an affair with Gretchen Carlson, a former Miss America who had turned reporter. We didn't break the story; we just found it in a local free newspaper. I wrote and produced a very funny and topical parody song about it which was played enough times during our show to make an impact. WRIC-TV immediately cancelled all their advertising on our station. The *National Enquirer* eventually noticed the scandal and published an expose with the headline "Miss America Stole My Husband". Well, this was too much for WRIC-TV and McGraw and Carlson soon left the market. Gretchen Carlson was especially sore at us and stayed that way for a long time.

Some years later, in Cleveland, Ohio, Jay and I were approached by a local charity and asked if we would allow a spokesperson to come on for a few minutes. "Sure," we said. The spokesperson turned out to be none other than Gretchen Carlson! Gretchen was so freaked out by the prospect of having to be on our show, she demanded certain "rules" be followed for the interview including no mention of the incident in Richmond. Jay and I were quite amused by her behavior.

What she didn't know was that we would have never compromised the charity's good name by cornering their spokesperson into a conversation about past indiscretions. Even though we reassured her and her people of our intentions, she couldn't grasp the fact that not only were we professionals; we were really nice guys, too. We did the interview and kept our word. She was nervous as shit. We thought it was damn funny all the same.

During the Persian Gulf War, we held a contest where the first person who could get us a photograph back from our troops in the Gulf with a reference to the Q-Zoo painted on a bomb, won $500 dollars. The winning photo said "Good Morning and Goodbye from the Q Morning Zoo". We paid up and slept well knowing it was fired at Saddam Hussein.

At the height of the conflict, we dressed up as Uncle Sam and led the singing of the "Star Spangled Banner" in front of a crowd under the big top at a circus that came to town. Only a radio station could think of a promotion like that.

We met or spoke with a host of celebrities including comedian Jerry Seinfeld, famed psychologist Dr. Joyce Brothers, actor Martin Sheen, race car driver Richard Petty, actor Wayne Rogers, actress Carol

Channing, and actress/singer McKenzie Phillips from the TV sitcom "One Day at a Time" and the pop vocal group "The Mamas and Papas".

But, the most memorable person was weight loss king Richard Simmons. Richard was unstoppable. He actually visited with us twice and the first time I was not prepared for his approach to being on the air. I would liken his behavior to one of those damn little monkeys you see in commercials or on TV shows from time-to-time that spring around from shoulder to chair, then bounce onto the table, then your head - all the while issuing a constant stream of noise occasionally identified by words. Aside from his frenetic behavior, he was very personable and as evidence, I received a Christmas card from him that year.

But, one of the most memorable moments was when James Doohan, "Scotty" from "Star Trek", visited. It happened to be my wedding anniversary and Chris, a huge fan, was still with the boys back in St. Louis. I asked James if he would take a moment and call her and he gladly obliged.

Chris: Hello?

James: Hi there...hello there, Chris.

Chris: Oh! Oh!

James: How you doin', Chris?

Chris: Oh! Is this really you, James?

James: Well, I certainly hope so, Lassie!

Chris: You are such a doll to call.

James: Well, listen: I just want you to know that I would love to wish you and Corey, course, a very happy anniversary.

Chris: Well, now you're a sweetheart...this will be my favorite anniversary.

James: All right, that's gorgeous....How can you possibly put up with him?

Chris: Well, I'll tell ya...we live mostly apart.

(All Laugh)

Corey: Well, you certainly will remember this one, won't you?

Chris: I will. That's the best thing you've ever done, Corey.

James: (laughs)

Corey: You see that? You're better than jewelry. I taped that! I heard that! In the future, no jewelry...just celebrities.

James: I love you darlin'.

Chris: O.K. Bye, Bye.

I later transcribed the conversation to printed text and accompanied by a signed photo from James Doohan, had it framed for Chris as an anniversary gift.

The Q-Zoo was a hot show once again in Richmond. The "Virginia Association of Broadcasters" awarded us "Best Morning Show in Virginia" two years-in-a-row. Jay and I traveled to Virginia Beach the first time to accept it in person. Guest speaker and talk show host, Larry King, presented it to us. Earlier in the evening, we briefly spoke with King and he had cheese stuck in his teeth from the hor d'oevres. Forget the award. That was worth the trip alone.

In 1992, Clear Channel Communications purchased WRVQ-FM and our sister station, WRVA-AM. Steve Davis and Phil Goldman were forced out through some unsavory political maneuvering by other people at our station. The management structure changed and once again, I was working for people not of my choosing. Jay and I tried to make the best of things but we had little respect for our Program Director or General Manager believing they were sorely unqualified and inexperienced. Alas, you must be learning by now that Radio management is at best, a crapshoot. I suppose management feels the same way about on-air talent. Never less, we plodded ahead because it was still fun working at Q94.

In February, 1994 at about 5:30 a.m. prior to that morning's show, we received a phone call from our General Manager. Roger St. John, our midday talent, had died during the night. It was a heart attack. He was 48.

Roger was the patriarch of the air-staff. He epitomized the good feeling that Q94 gave Richmond. He was always smiling, outgoing, glad to be on the air, and a person who truly enjoyed just being a DJ. I had known Roger for about 11 years and it was a terrible blow. That morning, we had to go on the air and tell the city that Roger had passed away. It was one of the hardest radio programs I ever did, next to September 11. We took calls all morning from stunned fans who reminisced about how wonderful a guy he was. And he was a wonderful man.

Roger's death was a bombshell to everyone's psyche. The station lost an important portion of its foundation when he died. His memorial service was terribly sad and after that, there was less joy at Q94. Nobody had to say what we all knew: nothing would ever be the same. Death had finally invaded what we thought had previously been off limits. All of a sudden, we all had to grow up a little bit more.

Everything was changing.

Being in Radio often allows you to hide from the inevitable things the rest of the world can't seem to. If the format you work in features Pop or Modern Rock music, it can keep you younger. You learn to like it. You understand it better. Your musical preferences aren't stuck in any particular decade. You find yourself doing goofy promotions and stunts. You get to act like a teenager when you're certainly not and the whole process holds you back from aging as quickly. But, Roger's death was a reality check and all-of-a-sudden, we all felt a little a little older.

Jay and I remained at Q94 for another year-and-a-half until we were lured away to work in Cleveland, Ohio. When we left, the morning show ceased being called the "Q Morning Zoo". A chapter closed for Q94 the day the last show was broadcast.

I was there when it started in 1983 and was there when it ended in 1995. Even with the bouts of bullshit we endured during he last couple of years of new management, my days at the "Q" were still probably the most decent years of my career.

It had been a pretty good run and I doubt Richmond, Virginia will ever quite know a more refreshing, fun, and light-hearted group of people than the ones from Q94's Q-Zoo era.

Thank you all, wherever you are today.

Chapter 16

When I first began this story, I thought the difficult part would be remembering names, events and moments from years ago. Surprisingly, details flooded my memory. It is the more recent events - the last few years - that pose the bigger challenge. They are personally painful.

In the summer of 1995, Jay and I were approached by WLTF-FM, a radio station in Cleveland, Ohio, the country's 25th largest market. The station no longer exists and believe me, all of northwestern Ohio is better off. What we did not know at the time of our hiring was that this station had already seen its best times and was on a slow descent into ratings hell. By the time we got there, it was being propped up through the memory of its previous success by a parent company willing to put money into it just long enough until it could be unloaded on a buyer.

We were the morning show that was going to help save it. At least that's how we were treated - at first. The truth is, we were the pallbearers and the people in the front offices making the decisions knew they were all on their way to a funeral.

I want to point out something here that may or may not be obvious to you by now. People in Radio are constantly looking behind them because radio stations can be found in one of three states of panic:

1. Dominating
2. Hovering or
3. Crumbling

If the station is Dominating, everyone on the air is worried he or she is going to be fired if his or her ratings go down. If the station is Hovering, everyone is worried they're going to be fired if the ratings don't go up. If the station is Crumbling, everyone is worried they'll be fired because the fact is; everyone *is* going to be fired.

WLTF-FM was Crumbling.

In my opinion, the place was now being run by a General Manager who was out of his league and a Program Director who was out of his mind. I wonder how it is I have been blessed to work for so many management mental cases. Where the Program Director in St. Louis seemed to be on his way to a hospital for the criminally insane, the Cleveland P.D. seemed ill in a more comfortable, safer way. I didn't expect him to stalk me, yet I would not have been surprised to see him wind up in a padded room one day, staring out the window and repeating the names of vegetables to himself.

The sad thing is, this guy had been a fan of our show for a few years, having heard Jay and me in Richmond while passing through Virginia a few times. He was giddy to have us. On the surface that sounds good but we should have known we were walking into trouble early on, like during our interview. We were flown up to Cleveland, given the obligatory station tour and then whisked off to lunch.

There we were: Jay, I, the General Manager, the Program Director and the station consultant sitting in a cramped restaurant booth. After some discussion and the regular pep talk about what a great opportunity this would be, they told us how important it was that all three of them agree on whether we were to be hired or not. That way, there could be no blaming anyone if things didn't work out. They asked for a few minutes alone. Jay and I physically left the restaurant so these clowns could make a hurried decision.

What a class act. We should have smelled their desperation.

Let me speak about leadership for a moment. When a leader needs a consensus to lead, he has stopped leading.

Remember, this station was in the dreaded Crumbling phase and each was operating under the extreme fear of losing his job. They all needed a finger-pointing excuse just in case more shit hit-the-fan. No wonder the place was on power flush. Not one of them had the balls to independently make a decision about their new morning show. They only felt safe splitting the responsibility up into thirds.

Obviously, there was not a leader among the lot of them. What a sad triumvirate indeed. Of course, in life things often look better on the front end than the back end. It's the actual experience which defines your perception, not the introduction to it. If I had the ability to foresee every hopeless situation, I'd be smacking believers on the forehead under a big red-and-white striped tent during the summers and passing around a plate afterwards.

They offered us the job and we took it all the same: $90,000 the first year with an automatic bump to $100,000 the second. We were tired of dealing with management in Richmond and saw it as a convenient way out. I guess we were partially blinded by our own desperation as well so it's only fair we accept some of the blame for what was to become a horrid experience.

When we got to Cleveland, the first thing our new boss did was hold open auditions to find a local girl to join us on the air. Anybody could apply. The changes had already begun. We had reluctantly agreed to this but let me point out that the company was already prepared to play Russian roulette with their morning show.

Management wanted us to do what is known in the business as a "Dick, Dork, Dear" show. It's a radio formula where one guy is a macho jerk, the other guy is a boob and the third person - a female - is the sweet little thing who comes along in every conversation and says:

Okay boys, now you've gone too far, so let me just shove my sweet soccer mom ass in here and smooth it all out. There: now isn't that better? Everyone can be friends again. Gee: let's listen to Michael Bolton!

Fuck me.

The girl who was finally hired for this role was a Cleveland native named Maria. And mind you, this was a role. She had no experience on radio whatsoever. So now, besides trying to build a new morning show in a highly competitive market, we had to train a novice while learning how to adjust our timing to a third person. The show became *Corey, Jay and Desiray* because "Maria" doesn't rhyme with "Jay". Mind you, the thinking behind this was just as thin as when we based the name of my morning show in St. Louis after a stupid comedy service.

Sometimes, there just is no good reason for why things are done.

I will never understand why Program Directors insist on hiring talent based on their previous successes just so they can fuck it up by trying to change them. Technically, the changes to our act didn't start until after the first three months, which is peculiar when you realize the ratings for our first fall book went up.

When ratings go up, you generally leave things alone. But, for some unknown reason, these guys began tinkering and toying and

150

screwing around with our act soon after we arrived and never stopped until the end of our run. Every day, another Goddamn meeting. We would sit in the Program Director's office for an hour or two as he shredded our show, minute-by-minute, analyzing it in the most trivial, useless ways.

For those of you who are against lethal injection, I beseech you: permit it for such people.

The first few weeks on the air were especially difficult because we were replacing a well-liked Cleveland air personality named "Trapper Jack". He had a fairly long and successful run as the station's morning man but when the WLTF began to lose listeners, someone decided to sacrifice him. Sometimes, the people who run radio stations act like superstitious natives perched at the top of a volcano more than willing to toss someone in to appease the Gods – whether they're the root of the problem or not.

Of course, after Trapper Jack was pushed into the lava, the audience still left listening was pretty pissed off and when we came on the air, their anger was aimed directly at us.

"We hate you. Die," pretty much summed up their feelings and who could blame them? Nobody wants to lose his or her favorite morning radio show or personality. All we could do was say we were sorry, tell them we understood how they felt, and ask them to listen to us for a couple of weeks before making up their mind and abandoning the station. Eventually, the venom lessened and over time, we did convert many listeners. Months later, we began to get calls from listeners who would say things like, "When Trapper Jack left, I didn't think anyone could replace him – but now I'm a fan."

You can't imagine how good a call like that can feel. Listeners are creatures of habit and the trick is to give them a reason to come back each day with fresh material while maintaining consistency. Unfortunately, that task was not helped in any measure by our Program Director.

The next two years were a nightmare. Every few weeks he would tell us we needed to retool the show. Revamp it. Change emphasis. Do more relationship humor. Talk less. Talk more. Play more music. Less music. Don't actually say the word "sex". Yes, they actually asked us to stop using the word sex. The Program Director thought we should use the euphemism "whoopee". Mind you, our target audience was women, 18-

49. Do you think for a moment, all those magazines at the supermarket checkout aimed at these same women use the word "whoopee" in story teasers on the covers? On the contrary. "SEX" is printed quite boldly every week on those covers. That's the sell. Just what was this guy thinking?

But, it got worse and I knew we were going down for good when the General Manager called me into his office one day and said to me,

"Corey, I know you're a professional and that's why you'll take this in the spirit I'm saying it. But, we think that Desiray should anchor the show. We think maybe women will relate to her more if she sort of handles those duties."

I said, "Are you out of your mind? She's been in radio less than a year! What are you trying to do?"

Remember the discussion earlier about how important an anchor is to a radio show? There can only be one and the responsibility of navigating that show through its 4 hour time period is not something to be taken lightly. It is a skill developed after much practice and on-air experience. Yet, they were willing to shove a novice into an unfamiliar cockpit to solo without her having the benefit of any lessons.

It would not have mattered what I said. Now I was sure we needed a second needle. Maybe a third. It was obvious the station was now being run by The Three Stooges: the Program Director was pulling us left, the General Manager was pulling us right and the consultant was just pulling us down.

The five stages of death are: denial, anger, bargaining, depression and acceptance. Jay and I had been through the first four already and by now, there was nothing left but to just accept and go along. So, we went through a phase where Desiray anchored the show which pretty much began a round of hammering. Nails into our coffin, that is.

The station was terminally ill. The music sucked, no matter how many hours our anal-retentive Program Director labored over his scheduling software. And our show was sucking even more because every time we got our footing, they would pull the carpet out from underneath us and change everything.

When you move your show to a new time period or a new city, when you add a person or subtract one, when you change anything significant in your show there is always a period of adjustment. You bounce up-and-down a little bit until you arrive at your equilibrium again. It's like trying to stand on a waterbed. You sway back-and-forth for a few moments until you find your balance. Every time we found ours, something was changed and we were bouncing again.

To make matters worse, I remained physically separated from my wife and children for what slowly rolled into over two years. It didn't start out that way. Originally, I took a temporary apartment while we waited to sell our house. Being a two-story, 4,000 square-foot white colonial home on 10 acres of land, it was the kind of home that needed just the right buyer because it was remote and custom built for us.

Unfortunately, it seemed easy prey for a burglar who broke in one day while Chris and the boys were luckily out. He or they ransacked our home, stealing my wife's jewelry and all of our electronics. Chris was scared and felt violated. She was angry, too. Not just at the thieves, but at me, as well. While I was off on another career move, she had been left vulnerable and alone to deal with the trauma of being victimized. But, the damage was done and the Sheriff said the chances were slim they would find the culprits, attributing the robbery to a crack head or someone else desperate for some quick money.

We became entrapped in a vicious circle: The real estate market was slow and months were passing. After Christmas, we decided the kids needed to finish out the school year in Richmond. When summer came, we put the house back on the market but then things at the station became unstable so we withdraw it. Back and forth, on and off, for sale not for sale. This went on the entire time I was in Cleveland until I was finally fired. My family never joined me and we lived separately from each other for almost two-and-a-half years. It was terribly difficult both emotionally and financially.

I felt guilty years afterwards about being apart from my kids for that long. One year after the Cleveland experience, I was diagnosed with clinical depression and put on medication. I couldn't shake the feeling I had partially failed my fatherly responsibilities. I should have been home. Instead, I was sleeping a thousand miles away on a $125 dollar futon in a small apartment in Cleveland, Ohio. I was sure I had scarred my children.

Some years later, during his second year at college, my oldest son, David, while home one weekend, confided in me that on the contrary, there had been no emotional damage. He said he never felt I had been far away at all during those years - at least not in spirit. Then, as life often unfolds in irony, I understood exactly what he meant. For he was now the one who had left home for school and not since he had gone had I ever felt he was far away, either. In spirit, he was always in our household and in my heart.

Love is the great eraser.

There's a simple moral here: Whatever you've done, it is never as bad as you think especially if you have a good heart and a conscience to go with it. Besides, there are plenty of people in life just standing in line ready to beat you up. Don't help them.

Cleveland provided some memorable moments, though. A couple weeks after we arrived, the Rock And Roll Hall of Fame officially opened on Labor Day weekend, 1995. The building itself, a $92 million dollar structure designed by I.M. Pei, didn't come without controversy and critics. It looked like an Egyptian pyramid with several non-symmetrical concrete growths on each side. A strangely odd addition to a decidedly blue-collar city where beers and pizza were preferred over wine and cheese.

We were part of "Radio Row", a temporary shantytown of dozens of radio stations that were lined up adjacent to the Hall, broadcasting live the day of its christening. We met some wonderful people including a then relatively unknown comic from Cleveland named Drew Carey. Drew walked up to our broadcast booth, introduced himself, and asked us if we'd play the theme from his new television show that ABC-TV was debuting that same month. Little did any of us know - including Drew - just how successful he and his show were about to become.

Drew appeared on our show two more times over the next two years and I was always impressed with what a nice guy he was. During one appearance, he mentioned he was in town to film a new open for *The Drew Carey Show*. It turned out to be the "Cleveland Rocks" footage which was the mainstay open for the program for years. He invited us to come down and be part of the cattle call for extras. We, along with several thousand Clevelanders, patiently congregated in a closed-off street one warm Saturday, waiting for cues from the director. Our job was simple: run like hell straight down the street when he shouted "action".

Right before the shoot, Jay was handpicked by a filming assistant to dress up as a fireman for the shoot. If you watch the opening of *The Drew Carey Show* sometime, you might see him. Look to the very right of the screen as the cast turns down the road and runs toward the camera. He is holding up a yellow fireman's hat.

An interesting line of celebrities graced our show during this time including: Carney Wilson from the successful '90s group *Wilson Phillips*, TV talk show host Jerry Springer, actor Richard Karn from *Home Improvement*, actress Grace Lee Whitney (Yeoman Janice Rand from *Star Trek*), rocker Meatloaf, exercise guru Richard Simmons for a third time, rock singer Richard Marx, actor Gary Sandy from *WKRP in Cincinnati*, and famous animal handlers Jack Hanna and Joan Embry. They were all delightful people.

In 1997, we crashed that year's Rock And Roll Hall of Fame induction ceremony that was being held at a downtown hotel. Desiray and I dressed up and sneaked in through the hotel lobby.

Before the event, I use my computer to print up fake business cards which identified each of us as a "Regional Artist Liaison" from Columbia Records. Of course, no such position existed but it sounded good and looked even more official with the Columbia Records logo I grabbed off the Internet. At the first tier of security, we flashed our bogus business cards. When they informed us we were not on the list, we acted quite indignant and demanded they figure out what was wrong. We were pretty brazen.

I said, "Call New York. They'll confirm us," bluffing my way through each syllable. "We'll be in the bar," I continued.

Desiray and I retreated to the bar, assuming we were about to be busted. Ironically, while in the bar, we ran into Jerry Blair, who at the time was Senior Vice President of National Promotion at Columbia Records. We told him about our fraud. He thought it was pretty funny (thank God for liquor) and didn't rat us out. He was impressed at how far we had already gotten. Next, we saw Steven Van Zant from Bruce Springsteen's band standing nearby. I had taken a portable mini-disc recorder with me for just an opportunity and we grabbed some audio from him.

All of a sudden, two security guards approached us and said in no uncertain terms that New York had never heard of us.

"Get out," they demanded.

We acknowledged being busted and assured them we would leave. They eyed us as we went through the motions. We had walked all the way to the hotel entrance when we glanced behind us and realized they were gone. So, we turned around and went right back in.

Back in the bar, we interviewed Jermaine and Tito Jackson. The Jackson 5 were being inducted that night along with brother Michael who Desiray later wound up getting a kiss from as he left the stage. It could be one of the few public moments Jackson has ever been seen kissing a woman.

We eventually bullshitted our way into the actual induction ceremonies. Desiray went to work on another security guy who was guarding a back staircase. She told me to find something to do for a few minutes. I'm not sure what she said to him but by the time I came back to where they were talking, he gladly let us go by. I can only imagine. Men: we always think we have a shot.

Once past the last tier of security, we were able to walk freely anywhere within the induction ceremonies. It was absolutely amazing how many aging pop and rock stars were strolling around: Michael Jackson, David Crosby, George Clinton, Jermaine and Tito Jackson, the funk group Parliament, the Bee Gees, The Young Rascals, and many more. We stayed for the entire induction ceremony, standing off to the side in this darkened but large event room. Nobody ever questioned us. It was great.

There's a lesson here that I pointed out a while back. As Coach Lou Holtz said: "When you get to the end zone, act like you've been there before." Damn if it doesn't work.

It was in Cleveland I created a satirical "Unabomber Screensaver" which brought me national publicity, including a blurb in TIME Magazine, April 22, 1996. In a story entitled, "The Web's Unlikely Hero", on how the Internet was treating Ted Kaczynski, the Unabomber, Joshua Quittner wrote:

...a third [website] gives away free "Official Unabomber" screen savers that include "fashion tips" and other surprises. "It's dynamite,"

promises Corey Deitz, the Cleveland FM-radio jock who helped create the computer program.

Ironically, my career was imploding and I was beginning to resent Radio. Maybe it wouldn't have been so bad if at least the job was worth it. Then, I might have been able to justify being away from my boys during some of the most important years of their childhood. But, it wasn't worth it. The price was too dear. I couldn't do the job I was hired to do, I couldn't get any respect from management, I couldn't see my family, I couldn't make love to my wife. All I could do was show up five days-a-week and be paid. Even though the money was good - what good was the money? I was trapped.

I began to hate what I did for a living. I didn't even know why I was doing it anymore. Chicago, St. Louis, Richmond, Cleveland. All of a sudden, every job seemed to be part of a huge gauntlet and all I was doing every couple of years was fighting my way through this ridiculous maze from one station to another.

In Cleveland, Jay and I became so despondent over our situation, when the show was over at 9 a.m. we would walk about five blocks to a bar located across from the courthouse, sit down and drink. But, only on those rare days when we didn't have to sit down for two hours with the Program Director and watch him put our show through a people shredder.

It never got any better. With the weekly changes to the show being dictated by Larry, Curly or Moe, we never achieved any respectable ratings aside from the initial first three months. The whole station was being sucked into a whirlpool of failure. Internal politics began to pit people against each other as employees realized it was every man for himself. The ship was going down.

Finally, the parent company, Secret Communications, sold the station to Jacor Communications. Everyone got a free denim shirt with the Secret logo that said, "Secret... a Great Ride", along with a nice big thanks, a so long and a fuck you. What is it with these corporate guys? In Chicago, RKO gave us a last check that said, "Happy Trails..." In Cleveland, Jacor gave us a shirt telling us what a great ride it had been. Yeah, why don't you corporate assholes get in the trenches for a while and see what it feels like every time some dick like you sells the company out from under everyone while you float away on your golden fucking parachute?

These guys shouldn't be running Radio companies. They should be writing greeting cards for Hallmark.

When Jacor got the station, they came in and gave us the same old speech about how the company was buying the people, not the station - the same words I heard in Chicago before the staff was gunned-down by pink slips. You could smell the death. Ironically, Jacor never got a chance to fire us because the station was sold *again* a few months later to Clear Channel Communications.

Clear Channel was in the midst of a buying spree, which had accelerated after the *Telecommunications Act of 1996* became law, permitting companies to own many more stations in a single market than before. Small chains and "Mom and Pop" stations were all being gobbled up by a few big companies and then the biggest of the big companies were cannibalizing the smaller of the big companies.

At the very top of this heavily-financed-buying-spree-food-chain was Clear Channel. Deregulation and consolidation changed Radio in America forever. The jury is still out on whether it was for better or worse and any discussion of it will no doubt bring fiery responses from both advocates and detractors.

Somewhere between the sale of the station to Jacor and then to Clear Channel, the General Manager resigned and Program Director was fired. We knew we were probably next. That's the pecking order in situations like this. It was obvious they had already started cleaning house. We just didn't know how fast or furious it would occur.

The Cleveland job degenerated and finally culminated in our dismissal in early September 1998. My ultimate frustration peaked in one final insult. Right after Clear Channel purchased WLTF I went to the General Manager and said,

"Look. Be honest with me. I'm getting ready to rent a home and bring my family up here at the end of September. I know things have been unstable around here. If I shouldn't, if you know something I don't, then just level with me. I can take it. I just don't want to go through the expense of closing down our house in Richmond, moving everyone and renting the home here if that would be a mistake."

Even if he couldn't come right out and tell me I was going to be fired, I just wanted a sign. Anything. A twitching eye. Drool. Anything.

He looked me right in the eye and said, "Don't worry. Do what you have to do."

So, I rented the house, put down a security deposit, paid my first month's rent, and moved my stuff in. Ten days later, the station fired us.

That son-of-a-bitch.

We found out we were going to be fired the night before it happened. The new Program Director, a cocky music-guru with atrocious people skills, leaked it to the Production Director while having a few drinks with him. Little did he know he was confiding in a very close friend of Jay. Jay called me up and told me the news. I was stunned yet at the same time, not. It's like a man on death row. He knows what's coming but when time has run out, the abject reality of it still shakes him. I called my wife to tell her. It was as if a long nightmare had just ended and I was waking up. I was glad to be awake.

I wish I could say I prepared for the final battle by standing in front of a mirror and moving my arms in martial art motions like a Ninja.

Instead, I sat down and had a drink. I was resigned to my fate.

The next day, we went to work and did a great show, even though we knew that at 10 a.m. they were going to can us. I know earlier in the story I told you that you can't take being fired too personally...at least not in Radio. But, being terminated still feels personal, no matter what the reason. It's the company saying, "We don't think you are worthy to work here. Leave."

Jay and I were determined to go out with our heads high. We decided not to show emotion or surprise. We weren't going to whine or complain or even betray the slightest hurt. There would be no verbal rationalizing about what had gone wrong, no last grasps at reversal, and no hints that it was traumatic in any way.

We had been though enough bullshit already and were not willing to let anyone humiliate us any further. But, they thought of a way just the same.

They actually fired us separately. The new WLTF Program Director took Jay into his office and oddly enough, the Program Director of our sister station, WTAM-AM, was relegated to dismissing me - like he had any right whatsoever to hand me my walking papers. I didn't work for this guy or his operation. All this did was demonstrate just how callous and unprofessional the whole situation had become. The fucking station wouldn't even give me the respect of being fired by someone I actually worked for!

My hatchet man began with some obligatory and quite transparent "empathetic" remarks on my behalf about "what a screwed up situation" it had been, the changes, the station sales, etc. Oh, please.

Hint: when the guy who is firing you tries to be your buddy ask him to shut the fuck up before he tarnishes the whole dignity of the termination process. The first thing people who fire other people think about is how glad they are it's not them. The second thing they think about is what a loser you must be. So, any "kind" words are at best, disingenuous.

After his soliloquy, he advised me of some end-of-employment details and then I was summarily asked to clear out my stuff and leave. In radio, they want you out right away. Like an unstable heavy metallic element, you become radioactive (excuse the pun) and they fear you will contaminate others.

As fate would have it, the henchman who was sent to fire me himself, was fired not terribly long afterwards under a rather scandalous cloud. I just wish I could have been there to express some "empathetic" words to him about "how screwed up the situation had been." Instant Karma is a bitch and if you believe in it, then you know there are no accidents - only the results of our collective actions. What you do to others, will eventually be done to you.

Jay, on the other hand, was offered the option of staying on as the producer for the new morning show, which would have been a step down for him. The Program Director, who had only known us for about 30 days, said to Jay, "Did you ever think that Corey was holding you back?" What a prick. That's the kind of statement one person says to lubricate another person's emotions in the hopes of looking sympathetic and concerned.

Jay was insulted. I was furious.

The gall of this guy to stand in judgment of either of us. He didn't know a thing about us nor our successes before WLTF, collectively or individually. He certainly had no idea how ludicrous and positively maddening our stint in Cleveland had been nor the real reasons the station was failing miserably. He asked Jay to go home and think about his offer for a day. As for me, I was given my contractual three months severance and shown the door. Once again providing yet *more* evidence that people in Radio continue to pay me for not working.

I drove out of downtown Cleveland for the last time and went home. I was sad but relieved, mad but glad to be done with it, and just pretty numb inside. I was emotionally empty and physically exhausted. I wondered how much more of this business I could take.

I questioned why I was still in it.

Jay was in a quandary. He did not want to stay at the station. He was angry with them on so many levels. But, he could not afford to quit. He needed severance pay and a way out. He needed a better exit strategy. The next day, Jay called the General Manager and said, "I want Corey's deal."

Isn't perspective funny? Jay could stay employed and I had just lost my job. Yet, Jay thought I had the great deal!

After some negotiation, they fired Jay, too. Hallelujah! He was more than happy to grab his things and vacate the premises.

So ended the last day of the largest failure in my professional career. But, the worst part of it wasn't being terminated. The real sting was knowing that I should have stood up to management sooner and simply refused to dig myself into a professional hole. I'm not saying be a prima donna. A prima donna is a vain and temperamental person. When you take a stance based on experience and reason, you're a professional.

The fact of the matter is, sometimes they are wrong and you are right.

Not recognizing those moments in your life robs you of the self-esteem you deserve. I would have had more respect for myself if I had just refused the incessant and baseless changes they constantly made to our show from the beginning. It would have been better to have just been fired early on for insubordination than to have lingered for almost 2 1/2 years in the shadow of their indecision and desperation.

It took me a few days to tie up loose ends and within a week I was back in Virginia. When I finally arrived and drove up the gravel driveway to my country house, I felt like I was Atlas and a divine event had removed the weight of the world from my shoulders.

There is no deeper peace than to be reunited with your family, safe in your home, guarded by familiar trees off a very beaten path. This, I assure you.

Jay and I were unemployed for 5 months and 3 weeks, but who's counting. We both had different sets of problems to deal with and it took some time for us to recover from it. Financially, it was difficult but almost worse was the professional implications. We didn't have much of a story to tell. We couldn't point to good ratings like back in Richmond and in Radio, the numbers are pretty much everything.

Nobody is prepared to take your word for it and nobody has the time to sit and listen to a "sob" story. It was two years after the deregulation of Radio and companies were consolidating station operations and jobs.

Plenty of people were being fired. Hundreds of jobs were being lost. Fewer positions were being filled.

We simply were not prepared for how lousy the job market really was.

Chapter 17

Jay and I finally settled on employment in Little Rock, Arkansas, the 85th radio market. When we arrived there, our spirit had truly been broken. Much of the joy associated with what we do evaporated after the Cleveland experience and we both knew we were at a crossroads, professionally. Our new home was a Modern Rock-formatted station which eventually evolved though several frequency changes to become "Lick 106.3"

We sensed we needed to make a clean break from the type of radio we had been doing. Call it survival instincts if you want. But, we inherently knew it was time to reinvent who we were and retool what we did.

We decided if we were going to succeed or fail, this time we were going to do it on our terms. And no matter what the outcome, that would be fine. We were convinced if we just had enough space to do Radio the way we felt it should be done – without the interference from Program Directors or consultants – we would have a better than average chance of making it work. Our new company, Equity Broadcasting, gave us that space.

Slowly, we began to strip away the old vestiges of that "Morning Zoo" type of presentation which I had been doing in one form or another since 1983 and Jay had been doing with me since 1990. We tossed out the stale characters, dropped the stupid sound effects, did away with the overdone "Top 10" lists, trivia questions, and anything else most morning deejays insisted on including in their act.

We moved away from the boring book author interviews, the "Joke Thursdays", the played-out stunts; all of it. After working together for eight years, our natural rapport, sense of humor and timing had become buried under old Radio baggage. So, we began to peel away all the leftover layers of status quo radio we had become trapped under.

Gradually we began to recognize that our greatest asset was ourselves. I know that sounds over simplified and almost corny, but it's true. It wasn't until we began to depend almost entirely on our natural repartee and individual wit that we began to finally develop a new and original show and most of all our own style.

Over the course of a year, we made a dramatic shift in who we were and how we looked at the world to interpret it for our audience. We started doing everything consultants had always warned us against. We dropped the bullshit and got *real* in our own funny way.

We came right out and told our new listeners we were complete failures. We admitted it often and told them not to expect too much. We told them about Cleveland and what an abomination it had been. We told everyone it wasn't that good of a show and we weren't even willing to try that hard. Jay and I came right out and told listeners the truth: we were "Nice Guys with a Bad Attitude".

We began to develop new "benchmarks" for the show like "Head Up Your Ass Headlines" – a daily compilation of offbeat stories; "When Animals Get Pissed" – stories of animals attacking humans; "The Really Awful Terrible Files" – a segment comprised of such awful stories of death and destruction, we warned listeners if they laughed, "they had no soul"; and the "Who Gives A Rat's Ass Report" – our version of a daily Hollywood/music/celebrity report.

The bulk of our program was a succession of banter from the day's news which ultimately evolved into a mix of topical and lifestyle stories, cyber culture, occasional rants and a penchant for what we like to call "hold my beer and watch this" stories - the type of news that's compelling, possibly gruesome, and when it's over you think to yourself, "Man, I'm glad that's not me."

Nothing was too personal to bring to the show. We talked about our imperfect lives, our pathetic idiosyncrasies, our fears, our joys, and most of all those things in the world that made no sense at all and were just waiting to be raged against by people like us. In effect, we put ourselves thought therapy each morning from 6 a.m. until 10 a.m.

We, of course, continued to play host to celebrities passing through town like rocker Mike Ness from *Social Distortion*, alternative rockers *Eve 6*, actor/comedian Pauley Shore, and even the Stanley Cup. By the way: it has its own bodyguard and you had better not get too close without permission. Amy Lee and *Evanescence* visited our show before they hit it big. The band is from Little Rock and we had a long-standing policy of highlighting local artists. I'm not sure, but we might very well have been the very first radio show to play their music on the air.

Then, something unexpected happened on the way to putting our careers back together.

We succeeded.

Besides creating a new show, we also spent the first two-and-a-half years of our time creating a radio station called "Lick". It started as "Lick 101" then the company moved it to a more powerful frequency it owned at 96.5 and eventually to a third and stronger frequency at 106.3.

Listeners followed us with each move.

By the way, when we were throwing around names for the station, we considered calling it "Dick 101" because we thought it would be funny to have a slogan that said, "If you're not listening to 101 then you don't know Dick". Unfortunately, being in the Bible belt, we just didn't think the market would let us get away with it.

I was the original Program Director and between Jay and me we chose the staff, created the imaging, formulated the promotions, and fused much of ourselves and our attitude into the product. Not only did the station succeed handsomely but also by the summer of 2002, four-and-a-half years later, our morning show was #1 in our target demographic.

Then, in early September of 2002, the station was sold to a new startup, Archway Broadcasting, for several million dollars. Archway had been in business two months when they dashed into Little Rock and gleefully announced at a meeting "We are buying the people, not the property".

Fuck me.

Here they were again: those inevitable words that always foreshadowed being fired.

On November 19, Jay and I were summoned into a meeting. The machinations that would precede our exit were beginning. The programmer Archway sent into Little Rock to run their new property sat us down and matter-of-factly told us our contract would not be renewed. We were, quite frankly, too "pricey".

Pricey is a word management types pull out of their no-people-skills-bag-of-tricks when they want to demean you and lessen your importance because we all know that anything determined pricey is usually something which requires more money than it's worth.

Then he started to tell us how much less money morning shows made in even bigger markets and suggested that the only way we could stay on with Archway would be for us to come up with "a way" the company could afford us. This was code for "how much of a salary reduction were you willing to take". He then alluded to a fifty percent pay cut.

We were instructed that any proposal we might come up with would have to be on his desk by Monday. This was Thursday. Meeting over. Have a nice day.

Jay and I talked about it and after much thought just decided, fuck it. We had #1 ratings and if Archway didn't want to continue to employ us when our contract ended, that would be fine. Cleveland had taught us the hard lesson of what it feels like to forfeit your dignity. That was not going to happen again. This time it really wasn't about money – at least not for me. It was about self-respect.

I was not going to bend over and kiss some egotistical programmer's ass who didn't know the first thing about the station we had helped build, the listeners we had nurtured and the radio show we had reinvented.

There just comes a moment in your life when you realize if you don't stand up now, you will never get out of the chair again. There was nothing to negotiate. There was nothing to feel badly about. There was no guilt. We had done our job well and were being compensated for it. We had a business agreement and planned to keep performing our services as required.

In the end, we proposed nothing at all to the Archway executioner and went about the business of doing our show and honoring our half of the contract. The plan was simple: work it out and then face unemployment. We could both live with that.

A week later, the day before Thanksgiving, Jay and I were relieved of our duties, told to get our stuff and go leave the building. By now, you know the drill: another employee was assigned to stay with us to make sure we exited in a timely fashion. Another example of how Radio companies seem to suffer from this bizarre paranoia, thinking every terminated employee will suddenly turn on them like a tiger in a *Siegfried and Roy* show.

I gathered up my things and on the way down the hall, I'm sure someone yelled out, "Dead man walking".

As it turned out, Equity Broadcasting, Lick 106.3's original owner, apparently did not transfer our contracts as part of the sale to Archway. That's not uncommon. Contracts transfer or *not* depending on the negotiated deal. Upon our dismissal by Archway, Equity agreed it would continue to honor our agreement and pay us to the end, which amounted to about four-and-a-half months. It was a gallant gesture. Technically, we were still employed. We just didn't have to work.

If I had a dollar for every time someone paid me a dollar not to work, I'd be rich.

I assume Archway was thrilled because now they could lower their overhead substantially. This left me perplexed because I had *never* known of a radio station that purposely disposed of a #1 morning show simply because they were well paid.

Most stations rejoice, hand out cigars and raise the rates for their commercials.

But, these people apparently had a brilliant plan for success nobody else in broadcasting had ever thought of: buy a highly successful radio station for wads of money and then slowly dissect it and piss away the investment.

What did it matter? We were out of the picture.

But, it was difficult to leave. We had forged a close bond with our listeners. What probably solidified it were the tragic events of September 11, 2001. As those awful acts occurred, all of us were fused together in a moment of shock, anger and sadness.

As soon as we heard news of the first airplane hitting the World Trade Center, Jay and I ceased our regular show and began reporting and commenting on the events as they unfolded. We had both been in situations like this before where the only behavior acceptable would be a cool-headed yet, empathetic professionalism. We stayed on the air that morning well past our regular departure and then, deciding there was nothing else we could do, quietly left the studio around noon to absorb the preceding few hours.

Often after that catastrophic day, listeners have mentioned how it was from us they first heard the news and how it was with us they shared their tears.

Leaving a radio job is harder than most. It's not like working at Burger King where you may have spent years churning out cheeseburgers for faceless customers. When you do an on-air job, you interact with people all the time: on the phones, at remotes, at appearances, concerts, etc. These are not faceless people. You shake hands, you laugh, and sometimes you cry. These are real people who you spend time with almost everyday.

The immediate separation is difficult. It's usually sudden and there is no closure. It's a very empty reality. Chances are you will never see or talk to most of them ever again. Imagine you woke up one morning and all the people in the world were gone.

That is how it feels and that is how it felt.

Immediately, a series of lies and spins began to be broadcast about our departure. The only way we could defend our good name was to post the true explanation of events at our website. As soon as people found out we had been let go and why, all hell broke loose. We were inundated with hundreds of emails from outraged listeners, and not just for weeks, but also for months. I can only imagine the kinds of phone calls and email Archway received.

Before the Internet, when someone was unceremoniously removed from the air, there was no way, aside from word of mouth, for listeners to rally to the extent they can today. Few would ever know why their favorite DJ or morning show was suddenly gone. With so little access to information or news, the event would soon fade. But, with email, message forums, and websites, listeners today are empowered. When a radio station or broadcast company makes a decision which directly affects them, there is no hiding from the backlash.

We created a message forum at our website where people could vent. The response was sudden and vengeful. A day or two after the forum appeared, Archway asked us through an intermediary if we could do something about the hateful remarks some listeners were posting. I thought to myself, "How fucking stupid is that? They just canned a #1 radio show. Did they really think listeners would *not* have something to say about all this? And how perfectly cowardly to want criticism stifled."

I think it just goes to the heart of how ill prepared some new radio station owners are with their own decisions. This was a public relations fiasco.

And there you have it. In Cleveland we were tossed out because we failed. In Little Rock, we were tossed out because we succeeded. It was so ironic and comical there was no room to even feel badly. And why should I? I was a success again. If Archway didn't want to take advantage of the audience we were capable of continuing to deliver to them, then so be it. We walked away knowing we did a great job.

Maybe it was talent.

Maybe it was luck.

Maybe it was timing.

Or maybe you can fail only so long until you finally slide through some kind of a career black hole and come out on the other side in a parallel universe where there is no failure, only success.

The day I was taken off the air, I went home and waited for my wife and kids to arrive at their regularly scheduled times. I knew Chris would take the news the worst of all. No job meant instability and probably moving again – the thing that she dreaded above all else.

Being married to someone who works on the Radio is a road trip for life.

Chapter 18

A few months later, while still being paid for not being on the air, Jay and I received a call from Dale Daniels, the General Manager and Ken Wall, the Operations Manager for the Clear Channel radio stations in Little Rock. They had an idea. We met for dinner and what they told us was almost too good to believe. They wanted to change the format of one of their stations and take a run at Lick 106.3. They figured it would be a slam-dunk if we were to become their new morning show. Not only that but they were prepared to help syndicate us, too.

We were stunned. Redemption seemed inevitable.

Jay had practically packed up his whole house, figuring a move was imminent. For my family's sake - and survival - I was seriously considering a solo gig in Tulsa, Oklahoma. After 13 years together, it looked like Jay and I might be forced to split up and fend for ourselves. And then, this. Call it luck, timing, or karma. I don't know. But, something somehow caused a series of events to intercede at just the right moment to change our lives.

We had it on good word our original employer, who was still paying off our contract, would agree to release us from it and even from the "no compete" clause in our deal. Without this release we could not legally work in Little Rock for one year after the contract ended.

After a week of discussion, meetings and some quiet negotiation, we inked a deal with Clear Channel and went on the air a few days afterwards. "100.3, The Edge" was born. Our listeners flocked back in droves. Word that we had been rehired spread like a California wildfire. I'm sure Archway was shocked. I don't think they ever expected us to be able to stay in the market.

In just over six months, our morning show along with our new station crushed the Archway property that had tossed us out on our asses. We zoomed to #1 in our target demo while the guy who replaced us dropped to almost last in the market and the station itself fell just as hard.

And the man who fired us? He left Archway within a year, ironically, on the same day our new employer held a ratings party to celebrate our extraordinary success. He vanished off the professional radar screens I monitor. And although Lick 106.3 hung on another eight months, it continued to bleed and eventually conceded defeat. To survive it was forced to change its name and start all over as an "Oldies" station.

"And ye shall chase your enemies, and they shall fall before you by the sword."
- Leviticus 26:7

Our sword was Clear Channel and with their backing we were redeemed and avenged at the same time. It was enough for me to forgive Clear Channel for firing us in Cleveland.

You often get to select paths in life but you don't always get to choose the shoes you walk them in. Sometimes we stumble, we trip, and we fall. Other moments, we go forward with a swagger of confidence, moving through the events that amount to what we collectively call living.

In the final analysis, we find that life is sometimes fair, sometimes not fair and ultimately owes you no explanation as to which it will be and why. The only thing we can hope for is that in the end, it all evens out.

I attribute my good fortune to divine providence and possibly even the patron Saint of deejays, Gabriel the Archangel, who I am sure hovered above me when I needed him most.

I have debated long and hard how to end this book. No matter where I stop, it will never cover everything. When I began, my mission was to take the experiences of my life and put them all through a "truth-strainer" so what I wrote could embody some excellent advice on life, living, working succeeding, and even dealing with failure.

Many of us never take the time to sift through the raw data of our days in an effort to separate the personal chaff from the universal truths we learn from life. I guess that's what I've been trying to do and here's what I know in a nutshell:

Life is always worth living no matter how badly things may appear to be going.

Striving for success in your work or in your passion is a worthy pursuit no matter how often you may fail at it.

Failure is worth accepting even if you greet it more than once.

Your dignity is the only thing in life you can always control.

There is no shame in personal misfortune, only shame in not recognizing the worth that each human possesses by the mere nature of his creation.

Failure is humbling, hard, and bitter. We rationalize and sometimes rewrite events to soften that blow. Failure is the world's attempt to convince you that you are somehow inferior. Even if the world is wrong, the decision has been made. Your only recourse is to not accept it and fight back.

But, luckily, failure has a built-in antidote. Failing keeps you a little angry so you will try harder. Failure keeps you a little afraid of revisiting how badly it feels. It gives some of us just enough dull pain to push ourselves toward overwhelming success in an effort to erase the vestiges of how badly failure colors our self-esteem.

And success? Success is powerful; you only need a little bit to quickly wipe away the sting of failures that preceded it.

Life, work, success, failure.

And what about Love? Love keeps you glued together, gives your work a reason, makes success a joy and makes failure bearable. My life would be so much less without my wife, Chris. My love for my children and recognition of their needs has given my work purpose and lent it meaning, even when I was sure there was none to be had. My successes were accentuated when sharing them with these important people in my life and my failures have been softened by a warm embrace, a tear of empathy, and the grasp of small hands who only knew it was time to play.

Am I saying anything a thousand other writers have not already said in different words? Hardly. Then, why is it, a thousand more writers will say it again, long after I'm gone? I don't pretend to know the meaning of life. Hell, I've barely been able to keep mine from falling apart at times. Yet, because either I have been around long enough or have just experienced my share, I have reached a point where I'm convinced of certain verities.

So, why is it so many cannot surrender to these constants? Why is it we need writers to keep reminding us about things we inherently should know?

The problem with truths are, they are evasive and do not always show themselves readily. It is as if the Creator plays some game with the universe. After all, what fun would it be if everyone knew everything all at the same time? It is probably a lot more fun for a deity to let truths trickle out slowly. This way, there is always a bit more "play" in the game. Some will get it and others will just wander around, randomly bumping themselves against the corners of life.

Life is like a pinball machine and God has all the quarters. Most of us have to work for our truths. Seldom do any of us go directly to the bonus round without a lot of time spent keeping that damn silver ball from dropping into the big hole.

As for me, I was caught in the Cash Cage for a long time. It was a personal prison I sentenced my self-esteem to live in. I pursued jobs in bigger Radio markets that paid me larger paychecks and then equated the salary I made with how successful I was.

But, there is no point in succeeding if the success only strangles your spirit.

You may think I wrote this book for you. But, as the last words make their way to the surface of my thoughts, I realize that in the end, I wrote it for myself. For you see, sometimes the only way to validate all that has been meaningful in your life - is to confront all that was not.

I am freed.

Printed in the United Kingdom
by Lightning Source UK Ltd.
101918UKS00002B/201